Fenner Fuller's: The Restaurant and the Man

By
Nancy Thompson
2010

Copyright © [2011] [Nancy Jean Thompson]

Preface

Five years ago I inherited boxes and boxes of memorabilia about our family from my mother, Mrs. Roy Nielsen. In Fall of 2010 I was able to begin sorting out this wealth of material and heritage. One of the individuals about whom I have material is Fenner Fuller, my uncle by marriage. The materials about him included: information about his family, his memories, thoughts and opinions, and his creative endeavors, including the restaurant he owned and operated which was called *Fenner Fuller's*. The information about his memories, thoughts and opinions came primarily from a weekly column, called *Gourmet's Corner*, which he wrote over a three-year period between 1961 and 1964 for a local paper called *The Times*. Typically the columns also included recipes he used or proposed be used by readers of *The Times*. While there may have been a total of approximately 130 columns, I inherited only 54, 14 of which were only in draft form and 20 of which were without a specified date. Nevertheless, this book has been organized on the basis of these columns (arranged chronologically as much as possible) with complementary photos and other artifacts about Uncle Fenner's life. The following page is an article written by Bill Masterson, publisher of *The Times*, on the first day *The Times* was published, which was also the first day one of Uncle Fenner's columns was published.

I am indebted to my aunt, Esther Torosian Fuller, who documented much of the information and to my husband, David Thompson, who has provided considerable advice and assistance in preparing these materials for sharing.

Sanctioned by Grand
Lake and Lakeshore
Merchants Associations

The Times

A Newspaper Deeply Conscious of Its Public Trust
Serving Lakeshore—Grand Lake—Piedmont

Wednesday, September 27, 1961   OAKLAND, CALIFORNIA   Volume I—No. 1

"Off the Record"

By BILL MASTERSON

We want to print as good a newspaper as we can.

We're not going to peddle a lot of twaddle about the self respect, nobility of the press and our duty to our public, or to speak a few kindly words about ethics. Those things, such as they are, are evident in our opening paragraph.

If you have ever had any experience with a fly by night rag or publication edited only for their nuisance value or monetary return to their editors, you'll know what we mean.

In any efficiently conducted enterprise there are 99 parts drudgery to one part romance and this is particularly true of the newspaper business.

Fiction and the drama have deluded the public into thinking that the profession of journalism is a dizzy whirl of tempermental city editors, cameramen who are a dare devil mixture of gangster and Sir Galahad; reporters whose lives combine all the glamor of Sherlock Holmes with the robust habits of Falstaff, and who lunge from adventure to adventure without pause for rest or sleep; and office boys who are juvenile prodigies of humor when they match wits with the potentates of the underworld. This conception of the calling of gathering and disseminating news is far from the fact.

The daily life of any man in the office of a newspaper is one of plodding drudgery. Owners have to meet payrolls and master the intricate problem of supplying enough material when there is not enough material to go around. They have the same labor problems, the same difficult overheads as the head of any manufacturing firm, circulation, gathering copy, selling space, maintaining quality, determining policy and format. It is intricate and laborious.

Your glamorous reporter gets his story and his info not by eccentric explosions of genius, glamourous accident or amourous adventure, but by doggedly following every lead, wearing thin the soles of his shoes, and assiduously cultivating every source of information open to him.

When you combine in two persons the duties of owners, business managers, editors, circulation dept., reporters, advertising sales, you have a job that leaves scant time for anything but demanding labor and wearing concentration.

We have tried and are trying, (not unsuccessfully, we are told) to be of service to this district by giving you an honest, clean, trustworthy independent newspaper.

Dedication

Uncle Fenner was a loving, hard-working, colorful uncle. Even though he was an excellent cook, on Mondays, his day off, he and my aunt often ate dinner with our family so that I had frequent occasions to be with him.

While Fenner was born in Rhode Island, he relocated (perhaps leaving home with a touring Chautauqua group) to California where he met and married my mother's sister, Esther Torosian, in 1929. The story goes that they went to serve as witnesses for the marriage of another aunt but, while in Reno, decided to marry themselves as well. Fenner had various odd jobs in CA until 1945 when he opened a restaurant in Oakland called Fenner Fuller's.

Even though Uncle Fenner had Fuller ancestors who came to North America with the Great Migration and Fenner ancestors who governed Rhode Island, he was without pretense. He was a dickens of a character but he had soul. Uncle Fenner related to a broad range of people- from homeless folks who frequented the back door of his restaurant to famous dignitaries, artists, musicians, etc. -with genuine interest and compassion. He enjoyed life and did not bow to the gods of materialism or political correctness.

While Uncle Fenner and Aunt Esther never had children of their own, (perhaps partially attributed to the fact that Esther had a serious chronic health problem called Familial Mediterranean Fever) he was constantly creating- whether it was enjoyable dining experiences at the restaurant or ceramic clowns. Once he took me with him to purchase groceries for the restaurant at a wholesale market in downtown Oakland in the whee hours of the morning. I knew that he would then spend most of the rest of the day preparing meals and then supervising their delivery to customers. When customers were at the restaurant, he was often in the dining area, chatting and joking with them, frequently shaking their heads while he made a strange sound with his mouth to simulate the rattling of their brains. Most of the customers loved this attention. Sometimes customers who had nowhere else to go for the holidays joined our family at my home after the restaurant closed. I think I learned my penchant for mingling at the restaurant. I have been told that one evening, while still using a high chair, I leaned over to the child sitting in a nearby high chair and asked, "And who is your babysitter?"

Fenner created many, many ceramic clowns at Mills College. Most look a lot like him. I was very proud to have him demonstrate his clown-making talents to my grade school class. At one point I was told that Red Skelton wanted to purchase a clown, but could not because Uncle Fenner never sold them to anyone- they were his children. Many of the clowns were used as candle holders at the restaurant and, at times, the clowns were on display at the Oakland Museum.

In addition to being creative himself, Uncle Fenner and my Aunt Esther were also active supporters of other creative people- ceramicists, painters, musicians, sculptors, photographers, authors, etc.. These included Milhaud, Bufano, Hagopian, Hagemeyer, Siegriest, Amara among others. The support was provided in the way of free meals at the restaurant and use of the restaurant as a gallery in which to display or promote their art.

Remembering Uncle Fenner and his approach to life has helped me anticipate more clearly a time when earth (as well as heaven) will be full of God's glory. Further, the experience of preparing this book has enabled me to use a passion of my own- organizing and disseminating information- which I believe is where I can best experience the joy of creativity.

Contents

	Page
Preface	iii-iv
Dedication	v-vi
Contents	vii-viii
List of columns	ix-x
Guide to the recipes	xi-iv
The Columns/artifacts	1-109 |//

Appendices

A	Miscellaneous recipes	A1-6
B	Fenner's death	B1-4
C	The closing of Fenner Fuller's	C1-4

List of columns

Date	Title	Page
9/27/1961	It's a shame	1
10/4/1961	Well folks did you get	3
Unknown	Last week I tried to think of the	5
Unknown	Last week while Mrs. Fuller	7
Unknown	At this time of year	8-9
Unknown	Wow what a lulu of a zoop	11
12/13/1961	Looking thru	13
12/27/1961	From Holland comes	15
2/14/1962	Yesterday, the 13th was my birthday	17
2/28/1962	Hello again. This is a day	19
Unknown	For the past six months (DRAFT)	21
Unknown	I really shouldn't be writing this column	23
Unknown	Last week a customer came in	25
Unknown	Another hectic week gone by	27
6/27/1962	In line with my promise of last week	29
7/25/1962	Here it is, Sunday morning	31
8/22/1962	Last week Mr. Gary Burgess	33
Unknown	Here I am basking (DRAFT)	35
Unknown	Yep, I goofed last week	37
10/10/1962	Let's see now. Last week the editor	39
10/24/1962	The reason there wasn't a column last week	41
Unknown	This column is so tasteless (DRAFT)	43
12/5/1962	I really get a kick out of	45
12/12/1962	Thanksgiving is over and I suppose	47
2/20/1963	I wrote a column last week	49
Unknown	Just loafing around the house (DRAFT)	51
Unknown	My last column	53
4/10/1963	Easter is here again	55
4/24/1963	Oh what a beautiful Sunday morning	57
5/15/1963	Adventures in good eating (DRAFT)	59
5/22/1968	Let me think now	61
6/5/1963	Through this column I wish (DRAFT)	63
7/17/1963	As you perhaps know (DRAFT)	65
7/24/1963	Before I give you my masterpiece recipe	67
Unknown	I sure goofed last week	69
Unknown	Gee whiz	71
8/21/1963	Here we go again, my desk	73
Unknown	Labor day, boy what a day	75
9/25/1963	Last night a doctor was in (DRAFT)	77

Date	Title	Page
10/9/1963	Well, the three wheeler did it to me again	79
10/23/1963	Hi there Harry where are you going	81
Unknown	Guess what	83
11/13/1963	The publisher	85
Unknown	Yes, Thanksgiving is close at hand	87
12/4/1963	Hello again, the editor is publishing	89
Unknown	This column is primarily aimed	91
12/18/1963	Another Christmas is here (DRAFT)	93-95
12/25/1963	How nice Grand Ave. (DRAFT)	97
Unknown	Hey there, did I ever tell you (DRAFT)	99
Unknown	Whatter you know (DRAFT)	101
Unknown	Gosh Old Hemlock (DRAFT)	103
Unknown	As our great American (DRAFT)	105
4/15/1964	Before I forget it	107
4/29/1964	What does a gourmet eat?	109

Guide to the Recipes

Entrées	Page
Baked Chicken in Clay	91
Beef Stroganoff	17
Boer Enkool met Rookworst (curly cabbage with smoked sausage)	15
Boiled Beef with Horse Radish Sauce	109
Cape Cod Scallops	101
Chicken Friccasee ala Lucius	49
Chicken Hawaiian (leftover turkey)	47
Chicken That Tastes like Chicken	89
Chicken vin Blanc	5
Duck	37
Fried Bass	109
Goose (not recommended)	87
Gumbo	5
Kansas Swiss Steak	103
Kuft'e	23
Lamb Curry	39
Lamb Shanks	7, 63, A2
Lamb Shoulder	39
Lamb Stew	35, 69
Lucky Baldwin Tripe	57
Meat in general	A1
Meat Roll (not recommended)	59
Missovlobia (string bean stew)	69
Mock Bat (chicken thighs)	17
Old Fashioned Pot Roast	73
Old Washoe Club Pork Chops	41
Okra Stew	27
Oyster Kabob	107
Oyster Pan Roast	13
Oysters Hang Town	3
Pacific Broiled Oysters	A1
Pickled or Soused Tripe	57
Plake	11, 19
Pot Roast	A2
Roast Rolled Shoulder of lamb	31
Saucisses au vin Blanc	43
Shish Kabab	A1
Short Ribs of Beef	61
Slum Gullion	1
Wild Horse Stew (veal)	13

Other

Appetizers
- Caviar Blintz...97
- Crab Cakes...81
- Kreplack...97
- White Fish..15

Breakfast
- Potato pancakes..73
- Scrambled Eggs with Tomatoes...........................29,109

Condiments
- Baked Cranberry...A5
- Banana Skin Jam/Zoo Jam...7
- Barbecue Sauce...33
- Buffalo Barbecue Sauce..99
- Cranberry Relish...85
- Mint Chutney..67
- Mock Champagne Sauce..A1
- Orange Sauce...A5
- Peanut Butter Chili Sauce Dip....................................107

Desserts
- Custard...A4
- Fruit Continental..25
- Irene's Upside-Down Chocoloate Pudding...............A4
- Lemon Torte...A3
- Pineapple Jello...25
- Rum Mocha Pie..A3
- Snow Pudding...A4
- Tart Lemon Pie..A3

Drinks
- Dikke Melk...15
- Thanksgiving Cocktail...87

Food for health
- Cure for Hoarseness..49

Joke
- Cook a Cop...33
- Three Wheeler...79

Sides
- Corn Cakes.. 15
- Grilled Eggplant... 37
- Hop Shoots... 45
- Peas... 19, 53
- Potatoes/tomatoes.. 53, 81
- Succotash New England Style... 75
- Thin Indian Bread (Narragansett Tribe)................................. 77

Snacks
- Dips.. 45, 93
- Kippers... 83
- Lake Merritt Caviar.. 45, 91
- Prunes St. Helena.. 71

Soups
- Zoop.. 11

Gourmet's Corner
By FENNER FULLER

It's a shame that the editor had to scrape the bottom of the old potato sack and ask me to write a gourmet column. Things must be getting pretty bad for old "Bat" anyway he heard that Mr. Carl Reitz, he's the man that used to teach international cuisine and is also author of a very high brow book about food technology? He told "Bat" that Fenner Fuller is the only man he knows in the food business that can put most any kind of food together without any reason whatsoever and have it come out tasting good.

Before I give you a masterpiece in the culinary arts I must tell you that before I opened my restaurant about s e v e n t e e n years ago there were very few good places to dine out? Since then the Grand Lake District can boast of quite a few good restaurants? Namely, Moreys and Chuck Coughlins on Grand Ave., and over on the east side of the tracks there is a joint called Oscars, ask for Johnnie, also there is a new one called The Place, I haven't been there but I hear it's wonderful. Just thought I would mention this to you folks to let you know you don't have to go to S.F. to get the best food served anywhere. By the way, don't forget my joint.

Here is the masterpiece.
(You Name It)

Before you put this goop together please check with your "Blue Cross".

I—Put very little oil "cooking oil I mean," into any old frying pan, slice very thin a few stalks of celery and one onion cook until it's transparent, about four min. Put a hand full of ground meat; any kind, beef, goat, pig or whatever you like best, brown meat slightly mixing with a large fork, add salt and pepper to taste, shred out side leaves of lettuce, the kind you throw away, add a bit of soy sauce, use your judgement, after lettuce has wilted, add two raw eggs and stir with the same old fork, stir about two min. Now eat it. I think you will like this "Slum Gullion" however, if you don't like it throw it away and I'll give you another dilly next week.

Oakland Tribune, Sunday, Dec. 17, 1961

Park Nativity Scene Lambs Frolic On The Green

The Oakland Park Department's famed Nativity Scene has moved to roomier surroundings this year—and the frisky little western lambs are having a ball.

Because of the MacArthur Freeway construction in its former Eastshore Park location, the set — including 16 specially fabricated figures— now spreads over the lawn between Grand and Lakeshore Avenues, behind the branch library on the Embarcadero. The two lambs and their mamas are the only living creatures in it, but they give plenty of delight to youngsters of all ages.

Regularly residents at the Santa Rita Prison Farm, where they are accustomed to having people about, the woolly characters put on a constant show for visitors— particularly at feeding time.

SPONSOR PROJECT

Sponsored by the Grand Avenue Merchants Association in cooperation with the Park Department, the display dates back to 1952, when sculptor-restaurateur Fenner Fuller and several other members of the merchants group decided to help restore what they considered to be proper religious emphasis to the Christmas season. The set has been expanded and improved until it now receives national recognition.

Gordon Mortenson, Park Department display designer, has developed the various fabricating techniques in collaboration with Fuller. Illumination of the set is by the department's electrician, Spence Bussell.

Other points of holiday interest featured annually by the department include the traditional 30-foot tree at the Embarcadero, just off the north end of Lake Merritt; a tree at Picardy Drive, between 55th Avenue and Seminary; the big tree at the bottom of the Snow Museum slope, and the tree in the meadow at Children's Fairyland, which this year is being decorated by the boys and girls themselves.

DECORATE STREETS

In the downtown area, 78 living boxed deodars with red bows border Broadway from 17th to 23rd Streets and Grand Avenue just east of Broadway, as they have for several years. Also repeated from last year are 24 deodars on Telegraph from 16th to Williams Streets. These are all sponsored by Retail Merchants Inc.

The Montclair business district is enlivened once more by 70 boxed deodars decorated in Early California style by members of the Montclair Business and Professional Women's Club. Trees in tubs the year around are adorned with bows for the season by the Montclair Business Association, and a half-circle of trees at the end of LaSalle Avenue has been decorated by Carl Welsh. Christmas spirit is furthered by 200 pinatas in the stores and by a busy Toys for Tots drive.

Gourmets Corner

By FENNER FULLER

Well folks, did you get through last week's column? By the way how was the "slum gullion"? I got a good one for you this week if you like oysters, "ugg". Most people don't like oysters but they did a lot for the Narragansett Tribe of Indians back in the sixteen and seventeen hundreds in Providence and its plantations, so says Rodger Williams and Gov. James Fenner of the State of Rhode Island.

Be fore I give you the receipe of the week I must tell you about the "Nativity Scene" the Grand Ave. merchants put up every Christmas time. Perhaps you have seen it in Lake Park near the Grand Lake Theatre. Well, this year, as you know the state has taken over the location we have used for so many years, so I had to sell Mr. Mott, of the Oakland Park Dept., on a new location. We decided on a spot in the park near the Lakeside Library. I only hope we can get electricity to it.

Did you folks know that this whole scene was thought up and built by the Grand Ave. and Lakeshore merchants? It is one of the few, in fact, the only Christmas scene that was ever installed in the City of Oakland that the public insisted on being put up every year.

Carl Ritzman, Lou Moglich, Art Middents, Doc. Johnson and many more men from both avenues had a ball building it.

Oysters Hang Town"

Use the same old frying pan you used last week. Chop fine some bacon. Fry until brown. When brown and crisp scoop out and put into another dish to be used later. Fry some onions in the bacon fat until brown or golden, place onions with bacon in the same dish. Throw the grease out or better still make a candle or use it later for seasoning string beans. Put some butter into fry pan and melt, now dredge cut up oysters into bite size, add salt and pepper, brown oysters and then add the bacon and onion, cook for five minutes then add two eggs and mix the eggs around in the oysters, about two more minutes, adding just a swig or two of sherry wine. Now serve.

Let's see what happens. Some of my friends say that this dish is for the birds. Well, I got news for them. I had some left over one day and I went across to the park and fed it to the seagulls, and you know what? The birds wouldn't eat the stuff.

Sketch Fenner drew of his boyhood home.

Gourmets Corner

By FENNER FULLER

Last week I tried to think of the correct name for "Mud Hens." The right name is "Coot." I know you didn't try them; however, I talked to the guy that feeds the ducks and he said there were some missing from the lake last week. They are hard to catch anyway. I remember when I was a kid back in Massachusetts I used to try to shoot them and as soon as the buckshot got within a few feet of them they would duck under the water. We used to call them "Dipper Ducks," any of you Yankees remember? I think that "Coot" is a better name. Cute Coots; say wouldn't that be a swell name for a cute chick. Say, Bud, that was a cute coot I saw you with the other night.

Speaking of cute chicks, I have a wonderful recipe for chicken this week. It's called "Chicken Vin Blanc" or chicken cooked with white wine. Really I don't use white wine at all, the reason being that there isn't any taste to white wine after it's cooked a spell. I use sherry; dry sweet, cream or any old kind will do. By the way when you cook with wine there is one rule you must follow;;; Pour out a generous glass and drink it, the reason being you don't want to spoil what you have prepared with poor wine. By taking a few slungs of this before you add it to the chicken it will make you feel quite gay and free and another thing, if the chicken does not turn out all right you can tell your wife and guests it was because you got gassed up. A couple of guys actually got away with this once, but it was a long time ago.

Before I give you my masterpiece of the week, I must tell you about Mrs. ——— up on the hill. She asked me if the turkey I was serving was frozen. Like the honest man that I was at that time, I said "Yes." She said, "Mr. Fuller, I wouldn't eat a frozen turkey." That was that. She ate something else. Two weeks later she came in again and asked me the same question and I told her I had fresh turkeys. Well, then she ordered it and said, "Well, Mr. Fuller, this is more like it, I just cannot eat frozen turkey." You know what? It was frozen. What makes people like that. And why make a fibber out of poor me. I've had these so-called farm fresh turkeys and to me they taste like the bottom of a bird cage, so don't be afraid of frozen foods.

CHICKEN VIN BLANC

Place half chickens on or in a pan with just a little oil rubbed on the skin side. No salt or pepper, just oil and not olive oil. Put into oven for about ten minutes or until brown. The temperature should be about 400 degrees fahrenheit. While the chicken is in the oven, grab a saucepan and slice onions, green peppers, pimientos and mushrooms. Saute these in about one quarter pound of butter or the twenty five cent spread for about five minutes, then add stock or water. About two quarts. Let boil for a few seconds, turn heat down and add a little cornstarch, enough to thicken lightly, add a bit of chicken base if you want to.

Now place this goop to the side and take the chicken out of the oven and place in a baking pan skin side up. Sprinkle salt, pepper, paprika and add the sherry wine, the glassful you should have left in the jug. Now pour the goop over it. If it just covers the chicken about one half inch, it's O.K. Now place the pan, uncovered, into the oven and bake or simmer it for about half an hour. If you have any sauce left over put some okra and rice into it and serve it as a gumbo next day. I'm getting hungry. See you next week if you're still willing to put up with this sort of writing.

Fenner Chamberlain Fuller II

Photos of Fenner at Mardikian home in San Francisco.

Gourmets Corner

By FENNER FULLER

Last week while Mrs. Fuller and myself were having dinner at Kaiser Center with some friends, plus about two hundred other folks we didn't know, except for a few, anyhow we had the Gourmet dinner; That is where you stand up in line and help yourself. It's quite nice but I had a feeling of sort of eating in the stock yards, something like an animal. There's something about it I don't like, something like the chow line in the Navy.

While eating my friend by the name of Albion said, "Fenner, I've got a good one for you." I thought he was going to tell me a joke or something. Well, it wasn't. It was how to cook, (get this), Banana Skin Jam. Well, I must say, it floored all of us. It came about when another friend in the party mentioned something about a couple of strawberries being in a jam, (we'll skip the rest of it for now) and this brought about the recipe.

I got to thinking about this banana skin jam and I said to myself, "I'm going to try it and make Albion eat it." I took some hot salted water and washed the banana peels, then I put them through a coarse grinder along with a whole lemon, added some brown sugar and cooked the whole thing for about twenty binutes. Then let it cool.

You know, it wasn't bad, just a little bitter, but I think if you added some peanuts it should be better. You could then call it Zoo Jam. Should be good for monkeys.

Last week the Times received several requests for my secret in cooking Lamb Shanks. Here it is; Let Lamb Shanks stand in running cold water for one half hour, why I don't know. Place shanks in baking pan, (not covered), add salt, pepper, paprika, tomato puree and of course a glass of sherry. Add cold water until it covers the shanks about one inch. Cook for about one hour in a three seventy five temperature, turn over and cook for another hour and a half, turn the fire down just a bit and let it simmer. Take the shanks out of the broth and skim off the fat from the top. By the way, I wouldn't try to cook 2 or 3. Wait until you have company and cook about 8 of them. It seems to work much better that way. If you do not eat them all, they will keep for days in the broth as it forms a sort of an aspic.

Next week I will give you some easy ways to make soup. Soup is very good for kids and you also, cheap and healthy.

Fenner Fuller,
the Fabulous Foodster.

Gourmet Corner

By FENNER FULLER

At this time of the year I can't help but look back at my youth on Thanksgiving Day; I believe they were the fondest memories of my life. It took weeks preparing dinner for our family and friends and who ever dropped in. About two weeks before Thanksgiving my brothers, Gordan, Elmer and Delmont and myself would go out into the woods and swamps and gather wild cranberries. These berries were scarce in our part of the country; however, we managed to get a few pecks or a half bushel. On our way home we would gather chestnuts and black walnuts. Elmer always took along his shot gun and he managed to bring down four grey squirrels. I remember Elmer let me carry the squirrels, I put them inside my shirt or blouse, as it was called. I know I got heck from Mama because I got blood all over my shirt, ferris waist, and coat. That's all part of the life of a great hunter. My sisters, Florita and Leora were pleased that we got home safely, however Papa was pushed out of shape because we were late for the milking. After we got the milking done, horses bedded down, chickens fed and the egs gathered, it was time for supper. You know I never did know what Papa was doing all day, we kids had to do all the work on the farm. I guess it was cheaper to have children than to hire help.

I remember Mama telilng me that it cost eight dollars to bring me into the world and that I was the most expensive child she had. Getting back to what Papa was doing all day, do you suppose he was looking for more free help? This particular day was Saturday and we had a big pot of Boston baked beans with brown bread, homemade chili sauce, apple pie, milk for me, and tea for the others. This Saturday Papa had a visitor, John Hines, and when we got home I noticed that they both were red eyed. It was the custom in those days for the Yankee farmer who couldn't afford rum, to let a barrel of hard cider freeze solid, then boring a hole right through the center there would be about two gallons of apple jack. This, my father said, he only took to ward off a cold. It seemed to work, it was quite potent stuff.

Before I tell you about our Thanksgiving dinner I must tell you about our cellar. It was lined with large granite rocks that were quite irregular. They were placed by hand because there was no mortar, anyway it was as solid as Fort Knox. It had a dirt floor, there were several

Photo of Fenner with his parents (Daniel and Margaret) taken in 1906. Fenner's mother (Margaret Ward Fuller) came from Newton Mearns Scotland.

bins, each used for the different vegetables we grew: potatos, turnips, onions, pumpkins and hubbard squash. At one end of the cellar we had two bbls. of sweet cider. Fifty gals. vinegar, and two bbls. salt pork. Bacon and hams hung from the oak rafters. Yes, we had a lot to be thankful for in that cellar. It was dark and musty and you always had to light a lantern when you went down. I used to break out in a cold sweat when I would look out into the darkness and see two green eyes staring at me. I never knew whether it was our cat, a weasel or a skunk. I was always relieved to get back up stairs where the bright lights were. A large hanging kerosene lamp in the center of the room, a big lamp with a round wick on the kitchen table and a small one on the mantel by the clock.

Mama and my two sisters were busy the day before Thanksgiving making pumpkin and mince pies. Mother had a new gimmick she dreamed up. Instead of mince she would make a pie out of raisins, cranberries and lemon, and she got a lot of raves for it. Papa would make the dressing and I would peel the chestnuts. I would eat about as many as we put into the dressing getting a very bad stomach ache. We never had turkeys, we would kill four or five large roosters that Papa had fattened up on corn. I hated to see the boys kill these beautiful Rhode Island Reds but it did give us all a drum stick and I still think a good rooster is much more tasty than turkey; anyway, we couldn't afford turkey.

This Thanksgiving I am talking about we had about 12 inches of snow, so Papa had to hitch up a pair of horses to a pung (4 runner sleigh) and go down to Lonsdale at the end of the car line and pick up three of his buddies. After much whimpering on my part he took me along too. I remember we took the long way home and as Papa drove by Luke's Saloon he asked his friends if they would care to go into Lukes and use his toilet as it had been a long ride up from Providence. They all agreed and I stayed outside wrapped up in a blanket minding the horse. They must have been in there about half an hour. I never thought it took that long for four men to go to the toilet. When they came out they were all laughing and eating salted peanuts. Papa was smoking a cigar, I guess he was trying to kid mother, but not me. I knew all the time what they were doing because I peeked under the swinging doors. When we got home the men went into the house and Papa let me put the horses away. I liked doing a man's job even if I did have to stand on a box to take the collar and hames off, in other words unharness the horses.

Everybody was busy in the kitchen, Mama needed more wood for the stove because the dinner needed about half an hour more cooking. She asked Gordon and Elmer to go out and get it. Papa, quick like said, "I'll get the wood," but Mama was wise to him so the boys got it. You know what? I think the boys knew where the hard cider was hid because their faces looked a bit ruddy when they came in with the wood. At 3 o'clock the dinner was on the table, eleven of us in all. Somehow or other we never said Grace. I guess the Lord knew we were all thankful, anyway he never said anything to us about it. We started off with celery, homemade pickles, a corn relish that we made, and chicken soup with rice. We all passed our plates to Papa and he carved the roosters. We had chestnut dressing, giblet gravy, boiled onions, mashed potatoes, and turnips, and Indian pudding for dessert. The pumpkin pie was for later on in the evening; anyway we couldn't eat any more after our second helping. I'll give you the recipe for the Indian pudding at a later date.

After dinner, when the dishes were done, we all gathered in the parlor. Florita played the organ and the rest sang songs, such as, "Many Brave Hearts Are Asleep in the Deep," "Old Black Joe," "Tenting Tonight," "Way Down Upon the Swanee River," etc. I contented myself by the fireplace looking through the velvet covered family album and trying to tie a knot in the cat's tail which I never could do. After many songs, a friend of the family drove up with his wife and two children. They were older than I and they joined the older group and left me to my album. Oh, yes, we had one of those things you could look through, at postal cards—I can't spell it—sounds like steroptican or sumpin.

About 8 o'clock the company left, Elmer and Delmont hitched the horses to the pung and took Papa's buddies back to the car line. Papa didn't go because he had to get up at 4 a.m. and start the milking. Well, that's the way we spent our Thanksgiving. They were pleasant memories and those days taught me to be thankful for every day you spend on earth. Make every day Thanksgiving and be thankful you are breathing.

See you in the PUNG.

—Fenner

Photos of Arlillie Suddith, cook at the restaurant from 1945-1967

Gourmet Corner

By FENNER FULLER

Wow, what a lu-lu of a zoop I made today. We bought a crate of fresh broccoli and my cook trimmed the stems off. She cut them too long and being half Scotch I didn't want to throw them away so I put the stems in the old Hobart and ground them up, added some lamb stock and boiled it for about one hour, added salt and pepper and thickened it with some instant potatoes and then some lemon. It tastes pretty good but it looks like something that might be served in a rundown poor house.

My advise to you is don't try it, smells up the whole place, anyway I'm going to serve it and see what reaction we get. I'll let you know later.

Well, Washington's Birthday is over and I hope everybody had fun, even the shut ins who couldn't take advantage of the three days off and go out in the country and see the almond blossoms. Now Lent is here and I must give you a good fish recipe, so here's one; it is called (hold your hat) **PLAKI**. This is a Greek and Armenian way to prepare fish.

You can use almost any kind of white fish. First cut the fish up into serving size, ½ cup of diced celery, ½ cup diced carrots, ½ cup chopped parsley, one clove of garlic sliced, ½ cup canned tomatoes, 2 cups water, ¾ cup olive oil, one teaspoon salt and ¾ cup diced potatoes (optional).

Cook all the vegetables in water, put fish in a large Pyrex baking dish, arrange all cooked vegetables around it, also the potatoes if desired. Place lemon slices on fish, add the tomatoes and olive oil. Bake in a moderate oven for forty-five minutes, served hot or cold. Hope you try it. I know you will enjoy it. Next week I'm going to give you another masterpiece called TUT-MAJ). By the way, while at the dentist the other day some strange lady said, are YOU Fenner Fuller? I said yes, then she politely told me she enjoys my column but she wouldn't dare try my recipes. I said, why not?. She said, they all sound so horrid. I just dropped the subject Another lady said my column is just so much "wish-wash." Is it?

Hope to see you in church.

—Fenner

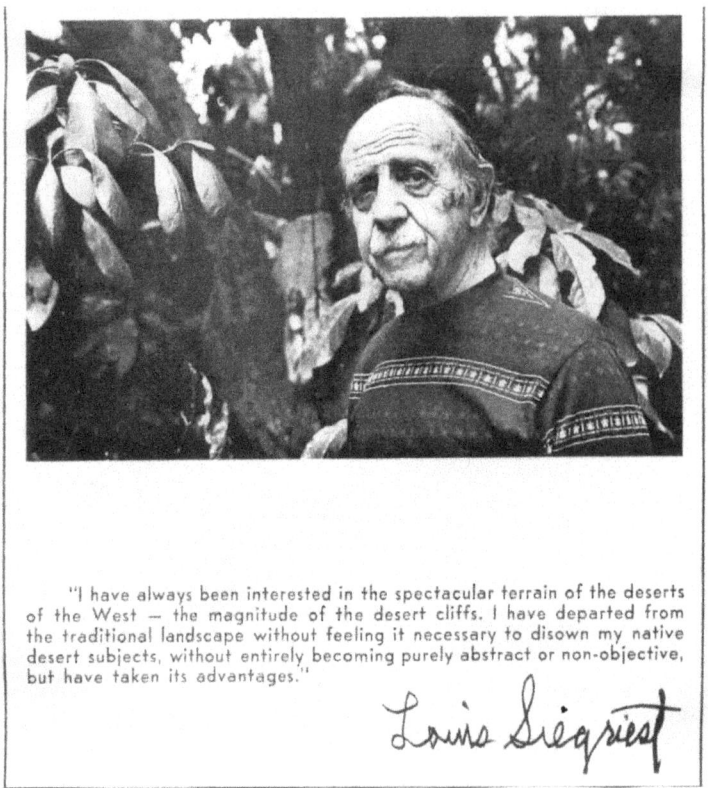

Page 5 *Louis Siegriest Retrospective*. Prepared by Terry St.. John for the Oakland Museum in 1972.

Photos of Louis Siegriest, artist and friend who ate at the restaurant.

Wednesday, December 13, 1961

Gourmets Corner

By FENNER FULLER

Looking thru the Virginia City cook-book, I find that many of my friends are cooks too, namely Lou Siegriest. He is one of the Bay areas better known artists. Lou paints the old ruins of Virginia City and is one of that citys better known citizens.

He came up with a whiz bang of a recipe. Get this; Wild Horse Stew. Just as Molly Crockers booze cake has no bourbon in it, neither does Lou's stew have any wild horses in it.

Have two pounds of boneless shank of veal cut into 2 inch squares, then dredge them in one quarter cup of flour that has been seasoned with one half teaspoon each of salt, freshly ground pepper and paprika Brown evenly in one eighth butter of fat, add one quarter cup of sherry made from Palomino grapes, says our artist, but that's not necessarily a fact that every cook should know. Also add the juice from a four ounce can of mushrooms and simmer gently for one and one half hours. Next comes a sprig of rosemary and one of thyme and twelve small peeled onions. When the onions are tender, add the mushrooms and a dash of tobasco and serve with steamed rice. Try this and let me know how it is. It sounds good, perhaps it is the tobasco sauce that makes it wild.

OYSTER PAN ROAST ala Mark Twain . . . When Sam Clements was working for the Territorial Enterprise back in 1862, he came up with this one; Melt a quarter pound of butter, to it add a pint of oysters, sprinkle with salt and pepper and cook only until the oysters are plump, which is very soon indeed. Pour juice and all over freshly made toast and dream no more if this is to be an appetizer, perform this rite in a chafing dish and provide little squares or rounds of toast to couch the wonderful oysters speared from the dish by the fortunate consumer . . . (Ho, all ye starving, hungry souls, Ho). From the Territorial Enterprise.

Last week I wrote about soup and I can't find the paper with the recipe in it. You should see my office sometime, no wonder I can't find anything in it. Right now as I look up from this old underwood, I am looking at old shoes, empty cases, clowns, pots, a few pictures, a Henri Matise scales, record players, broken records, a red arm chair that is full of old art magazines, shoes on the floor and my cooks outfit hanging on the doorknob. Oh well, that's the way we live, come down sometime, I'll show the place to you . . . No charge.

Fenner Chamberlain Fuller

Photos of sheep in the Nativity Scene across the street from the restaurant.

Gourmets Corner

By FENNER FULLER

From Holland comes, BOERENKOOL MET ROOKWORST, or "curly cabbage with smoked sausage." Remove the outer leaves from two or three cabbages, wash thoroughly and boil in salted water for thirty minutes. Add 2½ pounds of peeled potatoes and the smoked sausages. Bring to a boil and simmer for thirty minutes or until the potatoes and sausages are done. This should be a good dish after a long walk along the dykes.

Let's see now, what will I write about this week? Oh yes, I made a few things the other day for a Christmas party. You might try it and serve it at your cocktail party if the party happens to fall on a Friday . . . Grind up some white fish with onions, add salt, pepper and bread crumbs, mix this with one egg and roll into small balls and deep fat fry them. Put toothpicks in them and serve with a dip. Real good.

For you folks that have no trouble with your gall bladder, here is a quickie. Take a can of whole kernel corn, put in a mixing dish, add salt and pepper, a cup of flour, two eggs, and mix it together to form a batter. Grill these corn cakes and serve with bacon. Perhaps you should put in a small amount of milk, I've forgotten.

By the way, when you cook the cabbage deal, open all the windows, or better still, let the kids cook it outside. I know they will have fun and the neighborhood should appreciate the fragrancy.

I'll be back in a few minutes. I'm going over to the park and feed the sheep. No kidding . . . Well I'm back. Did you folks know that I had a lot to do with the building of the Nativity Scene? I guess I told you before. Anyway I like to brag a little now and then, however, since we have added live sheep to the scene, somebody has to feed them, and being that Fenner Fullers Restaurant is right across the street from this scene, I am elected to watch out for them. Yep, I'm the sheep herder of Grand Avenue. You should bring the kids down and take a look at this sight. Not at me . . . the sheep.

I tried a new drink last night. I'll call it "Dikke Melk." Take a few scoops of Edy's egg nog ice cream and for every scoop, add one ounce of brandy and about two ounces of soda water. Put in a blender or shaker and mix. Serve in champagne glasses. Very good too.

Next week I'll tell you something about India curry dishes. I have some real dillies for you. I'll tell you about Mulligatawny. Look for it in The Times next Wednesday.

Someplace in this paper, I have an ad. It is a menu from our restaurant. I would like for you to look it up and be convinced that my joint is not a tea

Photos of birthday parties for Fenner at the restaurant. Lower photograph includes Louis Siegriest and Auntie Florence (Fenner's sister Florita?) seated next to Uncle Fenner.

Gourmets Corner

By FENNER FULLER

Yesterday, the 13th, was my birthday. We had a group of our friends in for dinner and had a nice party. Gee what a head I have this morning.

You know, I am not supposed to indulge in any liquid libations but I did anyway. I sneaked a little vodka thinking my wife wouldn't catch on, but she did. My eyes get glassy when I take a drink and it is a sure give away. However, she couldn't say too much in front of our guests so I got away with it this time. This morning I have a headache, not a bad one, just over one eye.

My friend Albion was one of our guests last night (he's the guy who gave me the receipt for banana skin jam) and he came up with this one, "Mock Bat."

Of course it is hard to find a real bat, so you have to substitute chicken thighs. You are supposed to take the bone out and stuff it with dressing made up of bread crumbs, parsley, celery, onions and currants, salt, pepper and moisten with chablis wine. Then bake them with butter. Takes about one hour. Wonder why he calls it Mock Bat? Anyway it's new.

For my birthday dinner we had Boeuf Stroganoff with cracked wheat. I'll tell you how to make a delicious stroganoff. Slice good beef very thin, braise it in a heavy frying pan. When the meat is brown, add about three onions sliced very thin, add salt, pepper, dry mustard, ground ginger, lemon peel, a cup of wine vinegar, a dash of sugar and let it simmer for about half an hour. Thicken it with just a bit of corn starch and just before serving, fold in some sour cream or yogurt. Very good.

It was rather nice having dinner with my friends. Didn't have to get up from the table once. Our waitresses did all the work and did a wonderful job. Speaking of waitresses, I have often wondered why a great deal of people look down their patrician noses at waitresses. Really if you knew them, you would have different opinions of them. They not only have to have a clean bill of health, they have to be able to do book work, clear tables, serve you and be pleasant at all times even when some wise guy tries to give them a bad time. They take all insults with a smile because the boss says the customer is always right. Most of the girls I know that do waitress work are from fine families and most of them are keeping their own homes and putting their children through school. If you think it isn't a hard job, you just try serving a hundred people in four hours sometime. My hat goes off to them. Sometimes you might feel that you got poor service from a waitress. It isn't always their fault, the fault may lie in the kitchen. Either the cook didn't put up your order right or it isn't the way the waitress thinks it ought to be to suit you. They think of the customers' needs first, last and always. Now I'll get off my soap box and say that my good word of the day is, "Be kind and thoughtful to the people that serve you."

—Fenner Chamberlain Fuller

Photo of Fenner's birthplace in Cumberland, Rhode Island. He was born Jan 13, 1902.

Gourmets Corner

By FENNER FULLER

Hello again. This is a day that my peanut brain just can't figure out what to write about. I never realized haw many people read this column and it's fantastic how many dear hearts tell me they enjoy it and to keep on writing it. A great many readers tell me not to submit so many recipes, others tell me to write lots of jokes until I am really stumped. If I wrote the kind of jokes I know, the Times couldn't print them. My jokes are for the Whiz Bang or Playboy magazines so I guess I'll have to stick to the recipes and please most of the readers.

If you have any good ideas for a better column, address them to me at Fenner Fullers Restaurant or send them to me care of The Times, 3298 Lakeshore Ave., Oakland 10.

Speaking of jokes, this is a true story, but it has overtones of humor connected with it, so I thought I would relay it to you for what you might think it is worth as reading copy. Back where I was born in Cumberland, Rhode Island, we were brought up on a farm. We had a man working for us by the name of Persey. One day he was hitching up the team to go to town to get a load of brewery grain for our hogs. Before he left he asked my father if he might have a sandwich. My father who was blessed with a weird sense of humor went into the house and prepared a sandwich for him. He buttered 2 slices of bread and upon impulse sliced some yellow laundry soap into very thin slices and inserted it between the slices of bread. He then spread a little mustard on it and took it out to Persey.

Handing it to him, he said, "Here, Persey, is a cheese sandwich for you." Well Persey took a big working man's bite out of it and started chewing it until suds started coming out of his mouth. Persey got a startled look on his face and hollered, "What the ———— is this anyhow," and threw the sandwich in my father's face before my poor father had a chance to tell him it was just a joke. Persey hit the horses so hard they broke the traces and bolted all over the yard. Well, it's only a family story and maybe it isn't funny to most of you folks, but I just thought I would tell you what kind of a family I come from.

For you folks who like fish, here is a recipe I discovered about three weeks ago: Place as many slices of Filet of Rock Cod in a baking pan as you like, and sprinkle with salt, pepper and paprika. Slice very thin onions, solid pack tomatoes, parsley, sliced lemons, some white wine and a quarter cup of oil, and then add water until it covers the top of the filets. Bake in an oven for about 45 minutes. This is called Plake. I know you will like it even if you think you don't like fish.

Last week I wrote about the excellence of waitresses and you know what? The local waitress union wants several copies of it to publish nationally. They think I am great. I never realized by telling the truth what an impact it has. Really, I meant every word of it. And another thing: the men who wash the dishes in restaurants, most of them are great also. I call them sanitary engineers.

Just think: If you were to get a glass with lipstick on it or a dirty set of silver, you would tell all your friends what a dirty place it was to eat and a restaurant could go out of business in no time. If a cook were to do your steak too well or add too much salt or pepper to the soup, the waitress takes it back and he does it over again until you are satisfied, but a dirty glass or silver would send you away never to return, so I say the dishwasher is a very important asset to any restaurant.

Here's a good one for you: Put a gill or two of olive oil into a frying pan, chop an onion up fine and saute the onion until golden brown. Add one can of peas and heat. Add salt, pepper and just a dash of sugar and you have a real treat for you folks that don't like peas.

As the old Ranger says, so long until next week.

—fenner c. fuller

Photos of the Fuller farm possibly before Fenner was Born. The farm was owned by Fenner's grandfather. Eventually Fenner inherited it from his sister Florita in the mid 1950's. Fenner was the youngest child. His older siblings were:
Gordon, 1893-1966, Florita (1894-1955), Elmer (1896), Delmont (1898), and Leora (1900) .

GOURMET CORNER
BY
FENNER FULLER

For the past six months of writing this column for the times Iv'e had a ball and I must say, very enjoyable. Now my dear hearts, a great many readers have called me and said, "Fenner why the devil don't you write a book, thats a laugh, because I don't beleive that I have read eight or ten books in my life with the exceptions of the ones I had to read when going to school, and I must say it was rather dull, all my life I have been making a book and I want to tell you its been very thrilling, all that I have to do is find a comfortable place to lay down and just think of some of the things that has happened in my life and just think and beleive me some of the happenings would make my friend Henery Miller's Tropic of Cancer sound like a Sunday School paper, Of course some of my friends have told me stories that would make your hair stand on end and their life is good thinking. Some folks tell the truth and some tell me lies, of course the lies are not to hurt my feelings, but when my peanut brain starts to work, which is very often I twist their lies into my own verson and that too becomes a good book, if one daiped to print it. As to writing a book, where in the world would you start? something like this, I am the youngest of six children, Love and broken heart of a poor good looking but dumb kid, Necking in a canoe, or my love making in a canoe with soggy pillows, there are hundreds of ways to start a book but what is the best way? Perhaps I should tell you about when I was a kid on the farm back in Rhode Island, I being the youngest, I was the last to take a bath in an old wooden wash tub that my grandfather made by had, Mama would put the tub in front of the kitchen stove and open the kitchen oven door, as I remember your belly would be pink with the heat of the old stove and you fanny would be all goose pimples from the cold wind that was blowing outside sneaking through the crack at the bottom of the door. Gosh it was cold in our house, beleive me it was so cold that The thunder jugs or mugs or just plain"P" pots would freeze under the bed, we had what we called a commode to put the pots in but that was too much of a task, besides the doors wouldn't open, all warped out of shape I guess. as I grew a little older say six or seven, it was my job to empty these mugs and If you don't think that is a job just try it some time, there again my great brain started to work, I would line the mugs up against the south side of the wood shed and let the sun thaw it out a bit, then I would turn them upside down and in about an hour these beautiful disks would fall out, I couldn't resist scaleing them, I would put my mittens on, made of old socks, and I would scale these disks as far as I could and come as close to the Privey as I could, I got plenty H... from my father for doing it but it was something differant to do on a lonely farm, besides I think that I hold the record for the champion "P" slinger alive. Of course I thought of putting them on the back of the stove but Mama wouldn't go for that jazz.

Should I tell you about the house I was born in , my grandfather was born there too and he was born in 1829, quite a guy, use tell me tall tails about Abraham Lincoln, just think I planted potatoes and corn with a man who knew Lincoln well enough to call him Abe, Oh well thats another story. The house was over two hundred years old and is still stadning and people living in it, another job was trimming the wicks in the keorsene lamps also cleaning the lamp chimneys, I hated that job but I had to do it becaus e my hands were the smallest in the family at that time, another job was to darken the house in the summer time and then we would cut some branches from the oak trees and start in the parlor, that was room for company and where we keeped the old organ that my sister would play every sunday and some of the neighbors would come and sing , asleea Asleep in the Deep or some other cladis of the 1902 era, anyway we would leave the kitchen dood open and chase all the flies out, it was real nice to be without flies for

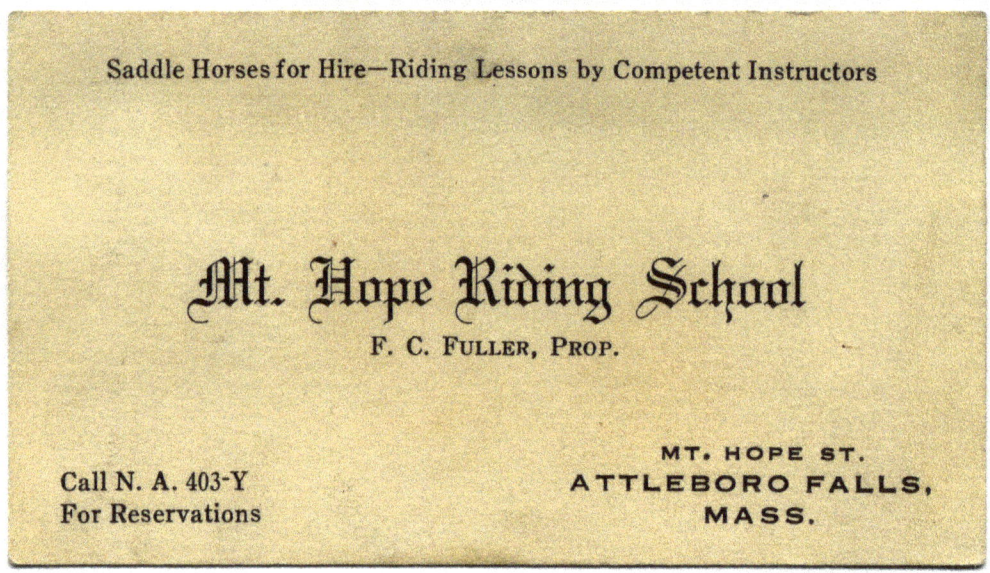

Photo of Fenner riding a horse on the farm. Evidently Fenner was a riding instructor at one time and had business cards to prove it.

Gourmet Corner

By FENNER FULLER

I really shouldn't be writing this column because I'm in no mood for love today. However, the editor might call any second now and give me heck for being late, anyway here goes. Can't help thinking about all the swank motels that have sprung up in Oakland the past year or so. Wonder where all the dough comes from to build such nice places. I know there isn't that kind of money in the eating business. It looks like a tax write off for some rich guys who would rather lose it in the restaurant business than to give it to Uncle Sam. I do know a few doctors and lawyers that buy ranches just to lose money. They have large holdings in the country and on week ends they don levy's and cowboy boots and they can't even ride a horse; anyway they have fun spending money for nothing. They really make it hard for the real farmer.

Enough of this rambling about nothing so let's eat. (Kuft'e). Get your meat grinder out and grind up some lamb stew meat. While grinding the meat add some parsley, onions, and some canned tomatoes, juice and all. Mix together, adding salt, pepper and a pinch of sweet basil. Form into any shape and place in a baking dish and bake for about half hour. There might be some fat from the meat so throw it away, not the KUFT'E, just the fat. There my dear hearts you have dish fit for a king. What king? The King of Siam, of course.

Looking through the Virginia City Cook Book I noticed that the first bath tub in the town was gorgeously decorated with blue morning glories, and was one of the sights to see in Virginia City. I wonder if they meant when somebody was taking a bath? I'm in a hurry so will cut this column short, so until next week I'll be seeing you in the bath tub.

—Fenner

Photos of a visit Fenner's father, Daniel, made to visit Fullers who had relocated to Merced, CA. Top photo is of Daniel, Fenner and a Jeanie Fuller Schofield. Bottom photo is of Daniel.

Gourmet Corner

By FENNER FULLER

Last week a customer came in who just got back from Europe and he told me about Fruit Continental. You take a can of peaches and pour the syrup out and fill the can with Bergundy wine and let it stand in the refrigerator for a few hours and then serve it for dessert. I tried it and it was real good. Try it when you don't want too heavy a dessert.

Another thing I copied out of the trade papers was: Open a can of sliced pineapple and pour out the juice. Then fill the can with your favorite jello, let it cool, take the can opener, cut open the bottom of the can and push the dessert out. I haven't tried this deal, but it looks and sounds delicious.

By the way, I noticed that the Park Department cut the weeds across from the Grand Lake Theatre and the surrounding area. Do you suppose we had anything to do with this? If you folks happen to be walking down around the Lakeview library you must not fail to notice the beautiful flowers that the Park Dept. planted. They used real good taste and it's worth a drive around there to see them. So there, Commissioners, you're not all bad after all.

Mrs. Fuller and I went out to the great music festival at Mills College and on the way out there we stopped at Dick's Armenian Grill. It's a small place and Dick and his wife run it and do all the cooking. It's just a counter and a few booths but the Pilaf was wonderful, and the Kufte, and the stuffed cabbage, and the shish kebab, and the so on, and so on, and so on, etc. It's worth a try but please don't get the habit and stay away from my place for my sake. The place is on MacArthur in the Dimond district across from the Horseshoe Restaurant. The cost was $1.60.

I'm writing this column a few days early, reason being, I'm going to a wedding in Merced, Sunday, so I will be quite rushed next Monday. Mothers and Dads of Piedmont Boy Scouts will be in my place that day and I'll be cooking all day long. I expect about 60 people.

By the way, if you fix that peach deal may I suggest Alberta peaches. So peaches and cream to you for the rest of your life.

FENNER.

Photo of the journey from Boston to Merced in a Mitchell touring car. It was taken in a petrified forest on Oct 19, 1914. The man in the foreground is Fenner's uncle, Willie. Others in the party were Fenner and Celina Chamberlin Fuller.

Top photo is of Fenner's brothers Elmer and Gordon in Brewster on an Easter Sunday morning. The bottom photo is of Elmer.

Gourmet Corner

By FENNER FULLER

Another hectic week gone by and here it is Monday already. What a week it was.

Still it could be worse.

Take my brother Gordon for instance. He was an engraver of fine jewelry. About the time he really got going good in business all the manufacturers started putting designs on jewelry by machinery.

Also brother Delmont. He learned the lace weaving trade and when he completed his training people stopped using lace curtains.

And then there was Elmer. He used to punch holes in horseshoes and you know what happened to the horses.

I guess I can't complain too much. I don't know what I'll do when people stop eating.

Speaking of eating, have you tried this recipe? It's called OKRA STEW. Use one pound lamb stew meat, two large onions sliced, one pound okra, fresh or canned, ½ lb. tomatoes cut in small pieces, one lemon, three cups of water, salt and pepper to taste. Braise meat until brown. Add onions and cook ten minutes, add okra, tomatoes and water cover and cook for twenty minutes more. Should be cooked about one hour.

About that wedding. I hate to be gabby but can you feature people that have loads of dough using plastic forks and paper plates when they have good sterling. Three jugs of champagne for punch that had to serve fifty people. Boy, how tight can they get? These are some of my own folks I'm talking about, so I'm keeping the gossip in the family.

It's too bad the fireworks won't be shown around the lake this year; they're going to be out at the airport instead. The reason being is too many (HOODS) bothering peaceful people. One fellow told me it would take the entire National Guard to control the punks. This is too bad. I don't know who it should be blamed on, perhaps part of it comes because teachers aren't allowed to spank children in school and it's a cinch the parents aren't doing it at home, so let's blame the PTA.

Boy, I'll bet I'll catch (&℔@) for that last statement.

So long for now, see you in the dressing room, teacher.

Top photo is of Mardikian ranch (Silverado) in Napa CA as of 1961. Bottom photo is of Fenner and George Mardikian.

Gourmet's Corner

By FENNER FULLER

In line with my promise of last week, this will be a continuation of my last column. Here on the ranch of my good friend, George Mardikian, we have worked out a very satisfactory arrangement as regards eating. George does the cooking and I do the dishes. There are no women up here (it's nice to get them out of your hair once in a blue moon as much as I love my dear wife) so we are batching it.

George Mardikian is perhaps one of the world's best cooks. He is nationally known for his culinary ability. George can put things together that will make your mouth water to watch him. Simple things, too, like putting a spoonful of butter into a frying pan, melt, add a can of solid pack tomatoes, chopped parsley, cook for five minutes, add salt and pepper, drop in two or three eggs and scramble with a fork. Don't cook too much. Served on toast, it makes an excellent repast.

As I said before the dishes are my job but in case you think I am in danger of getting dish pan hands, let me remind you that George is a very wealthy man and has all the trimmings to make a modern ranch so I do them in the electric dish washer. I also stated there were no women up here but I have to retract that statement because there is a Japanese girl that comes in every afternoon, makes the beds and straightens up the house after we have made a general mess of it.

Much as I appreciate his generosity in bringing me to this ranch, I rue the trip to some extent because I have been on a rigid diet and since sampling two weeks of George's cooking I have gained ten pounds back again. In another later column I will give you a real lulu of a recipe that Mr. Mardikian came up with during our sojourn at his luxury ranch.

Photo of Fenner at the Mardikian ranch getting milk directly from the cow.

Gourmet's Corner
By FENNER FULLER

Here it is, Sunday morning and 6:45 a.m. at that. What a dope I am for getting up that early. It isn't that I have to or want to; it's because my family got into the habit on the farm. We didn't need an alarm clock, the roosters would start crowing, the cows mooing and the horses would kick the heck out of the stalls if we didn't get up and feed them.

My job was to clean out the stables, wash the cows down and fetch the milking buckets for my brothers to start the milking. After milking, I had to drive the cows down to the pasture. It was fun in the summer time, but gosh, the winter. That is why I'm in California. Anyhow, that's how I got into the habit of getting up early in the morning.

This morning I am wrinkling my beautiful eyebrows trying to figure out what to cook today. Any of you folks got any ideas, send them in and I will try your favorite formula. If I put it on the menu, I will call you and give you a free dinner. For the past twenty years I have cooked Ham, Ram, Lamb, Bull, Beef and Bear and I'm getting tired of the same thing day after day. I often wondered if it wouldn't be a good idea if some farmer would fed his cows cabbage and malt beer and perhaps he could come up with a beef tasting like **KALBSBRATEN MIT BIER.** That, my dear hearts, is roast veal with beer, in German.

Woops, I just got a brain storm. **"Roast Rolled Shoulder of Lamb."** I'm going to roast it like any other lamb roast but I'm going home in a few minutes and gather up a lot of mint. I've tons of it in my back yard. I'm going to clean the mint and chop it up, add some sugar and wine vinegar, some old chablis we have around the place and make a sauce of it. Then I'll add some ginger and pour the whole thing over the roast. I'll bet it will be good. I know it will make a nice gravy so I'm going to take a chance on it.

Last Friday our dining room was jumping with customers. I don't know where all the people came from, perhaps you're readers and some of you may have been overflow from other restaurants on the avenue. Anyway, I was pleased to have you.

—Fenner

FENNER FULLER'S

NOW IN OUR 17th YEAR

At 614 Grand Ave.

Call for
Reservations
HI 4-9701

- LUNCHEON
- DINNER
- PARTIES
- BANQUETS

Advertisement in The Times as of 1962.

Gourmet's Corner

By FENNER FULLER

Last week Mr. Gary Burgess, a rival columnist who writes something called, "Bye Line" and Mr. Bill Masterson, the handsome gentleman that publishes this paper, each wrote about the three wheelers of the Police Force that patrol the avenues. Something about the errant publisher getting a ticket for an illegal U turn.

Well Sir: the very same week I really got hot under the collar. I parked in front of my restaurant and when I went to decorate the parking meter, I found I had only quarters and halves, no dimes, nickels or pennies. I dashed into my office, opened the safe and grabbed a handful of dimes and as I ran back out, there was the cop just starting to write out a ticket. I said, "Hey, wait a second". The cop just looked up and kept on writing. It made me so angry I threw the whole handful of dimes at him and went back into the restaurant and slammed the kitchen door so hard I broke the lock.

I should give you folks a recipe on how to "Cook a Cop" which isn't such a bad idea; he could be stuffed with old parking tickets, seasoned with salted smelt, wrapped in an old inner tube and sent to the Congo. I often wonder if Hizzoner, the Mayor ever wonders why the downtown merchants aren't doing any business. One reason is operators of three wheelers like this one. They should get smart and get rid of them. Oh, well, enough of that jazz.

I received a wonderful Italian recipe from one of you readers last week and I fully intended to publish it this week, but it is home so I will give to you folks next week.

For all you folks who cook out, here is a very good BARBECUE SAUCE: One cup of catsup, two tablespoons of wine vinegar, two spoons of worchester sauce, ¼ teaspoon salt, ¼ teaspoon tobasco sauce, ½ cup of chopped onion, one teaspoon of dry mustard and one cup of water. Prepare in kitchen; keep it warm until ready to use. Mix ingredients in sauce pan, allow it to come to a boil, then reduce heat and simmer for ten minutes without cover. If sauce becomes thick enough to stick to the spoon, add water. This is suitable with practically any meat.

Hope to see you soon,

2751 Buena Visata Way, Berkeley, Cal.

April 8, 1954.

Dear Fenner Fuller;

I want to tell you how much we all enjoyed the dinner you prepared for us Tuesday night. Somehow I felt that I let you down by not explaining that Rosanjin is a sort of "primitive", a Picasso among potters, and that I realize his work must have been a shock to you. I do not want you to think me quite a fool for backing his appearance here I think people should see and feel many kinds of things, not just one kind, not just the accepted things but the controversial ones as well.

I do not, at first, go to see a mans work to like or dislike. I go to experience and to think.

I do not say good or bad-- I say why-- and what is this person trying so hard to say to me and is he sincere. Does his stuff function-- not in my world but in his. This stuff commands my respect because it is the strong work of a strong man, his personal expression, carefully thought out and unique to him. And with that may I say again, thank you for a delicious dinner and fine host.

Sincerely,

Jacomena Maybeck.

Correspondence with Jacomena Maybeck, (daughter-in-law of architect Bernard Maybeck) who ate at the restaurant.

GOURMET CORNER
BY
FENNER FULLER

Here I am basking in the sun at George Mardikians ranch in St. Helena and it sure is a nice place to come to, especially when a fellow doesn't have to spend any money, in fact I tried to buy a pack of smokes this A.M. and he wouldn't stand for that either, so whats a fellow going to do? I sure spent a lot of his money this A.M. I bought four thousand bucks worth of young heffers, hoping that he can make a few bucks on them, however its just my luck that they will get sick and kick the bucket never the less, he goes along with my judgement and it makes me feel good. At seven A.M. this morning I went fishing and caught four nice bass, we had them for lunch and I must say that dear George cooked them to perfectin. I could tell you how he cooked them but I think I told you some time ago how to make "Plarkie" if I didnt, I willm tell you some other time. I have so much to tell you I know you are not intrested in cooking. Perhaps on the other hand you are intrested so I must tell you what Geo. cooked last night. Everything was from the ranch, grown and watered by his own hands, yes even the lamb. He braised some lean lamb in a heavy pot, braised it untill it was nice and brown, then added sliced onions, peeled fresh tomatoes, egg plant and okra, added just a pinch of salt and pepper and let it simmer for about an hour, I must say that it was a delicious dish, I like these things however you might not like it, but with taxes the way they are you should learn to eat nourishing food and make it inexpencive, remember Kennedy wants to get to the moon and that takes a lot of dough, so tighten your belts and eat well but cheap so you might try the egg plant deal. Oh. Gosh, I can't write what I want to, Geo. just had a man come up from his restaurant #with a four wheel trailer and loaded it up with tomatoes, bell peppersm, squash, egg plant and two ot other vegetables I cant begin to mention, well, it was gratifing to note, the guy that came up here to pick and take these vegetables said, Boss , what am I going to do with all this stuff, Geo. Blew his top and said, give it away you donkey, so# on and so on, turn next paige.

Fenner Fuller's

614 Grand Avenue, Oakland 10, California

THE PERFECT APERTIF'S
Your Favorite Cocktail or Bar Drink Served at Your Table
A Fine Selection of California Wines
Large Bottle 2.50   Small Bottle 1.35

Special Dinner
Soup du Jour
Assorted Relish Tray

Green Salad (Choice of Roquefort, French or 1000 Island Dressing)

ENTREES
Special Dinner of the Day, Your Waitress Will Explain, 2.50
Beef Vin Roque, Bottom Round Baked with Burgundy 2.85
OUR FAMOUS SHISH KEBAB, CENTER CUTS OF LEG MARINATED 3 DAYS, BROILED ON SKEWERS 3.75
Broiled Chopped Round Steak, Served on Oak Plank, Garni 2.75
Baked Rhode Island Red Chicken, Vin Blanc, with Pilaff 2.75
Broiled Oysters a la Fenner, Our Own Creation 2.85
Epicurean Dinner, Thick Loin Lamb Chop with Broiled Vegetable 2.75
Baked Shank of Lamb, Armenian Style 2.85
Broiled Steak Dinner: Soup du Jour, Salad, Potatoes or Rice Pilaff, Vegetable, Rolls and Butter, Coffee and Dessert 4.00
Broiled Loin Lamb Chop, Served with Pilaff 3.25

Vegetables and Potatoes   Roll and Butter

DESSERT
Exceptional Homemade Fruit Pie, Vanilla Ice Cream
Raspberry or Pineapple Sherbet

BEVERAGES
Coffee or Hot Tea with the Dinner—Milk 20c Extra

Child's Special Dinner — $1.50

Studio Dinner — $1.75
(Except Sunday and Holidays)
SPECIAL ENTREE (WAITRESS WILL EXPLAIN)
Vegetables and Potatoes
Jell-O or Ice Cream—Coffee

Advertisement in *The Times* as of 1962.

Gourmet's Corner

By FENNER FULLER

Yep, I goofed last week, too busy at the restaurant, quite a few large parties. A couple of weeks ago we had the Kiwanis Club and they had a ball. We set the place up for 35 people and 52 came; it was nice having the extra guests but I must say it's trying on a man's mind to know what to dig up for the extra folks to eat. Anyway we made it. I hope they enjoyed themselves.

By the way, we have a new three wheeler on our beat now, not a bad guy either, at least he smiles when he gives you a parking ticket. I hope when the overpass is finished that we can have a parking agreement for the Grand Ave. and Lakeshore merchants. It sure would be nice, something like the parking lot in front of the Auditorium, trees and all. Of course, the cars wouldn't be very clean after parking under the trees, you know, birds and all. Speaking of birds, duck season will be here soon and I think the best way to cook ducks is to stuff them with old fashioned bread dressing with a few currants and a dash of sage. Place the birds in a roasting pan, breasts up, rub with butter mixed with salt, pepper and a dash of paprika, add a cup of water and cook for about one hour in a slow oven. When ducks are done, add one small jar of red currant jelly and two spoons A.I. sauce, then baste with this sauce, take the birds out of the pan and skim off fat. To the sauce grate peel of one orange, serve with cracked wheat.

For you folks that cook out, here is a good one for you. While the coals are hot, place one or two egg plants on the broiler rack and forget it for about ten minutes. Turn it over and cook on the other side, then place egg plant on some newspapers and with a sharp knife cut in half and then spoon the inside out into a bowl, add salt and pepper and butter and eat. You can chop a few onions into it if you can digest onions; if not just add a dash of garlic powder. It has a very delightful outdoor taste. Let me know how you come out, there is a name for it but I can't think of it just now.

Hope to see you soon,

—Fenner

Photo of Fenner and his wife, Esther, dressed for a party of their artsy friends.
Photo dated Sept 27, 1958

Gourmet Corner

By FENNER FULLER

Let's see now. Last week the editor said I would give you some dillies for recipies. Tow the heck does he know what I am going to write about?

I gave him some good egg plant recipes some time ago but he never got around to getting them printed for you. They must be spoiled by now. Maybe he and his dear wife don't care for egg plant. Anyway, I'll endeavor to give you something good this week.

Perhaps some of you folks don't like Lamb Curry and the reason might be that you have never really had a truly good recipe. If you don't like this one, you will just have to go back to the canned beans and hamburgers.

Buy a shoulder of lamb and either you or the butcher can cut it up in squares about one or two inches in size. Then get a good heavy pan, place the meat in it and braise for about thirty minutes, pour off the excess fat, add two large onions, cut up and mix it good and cook until the onions are transparent. Add some powdered ginger, mustard, carraway seed and salt and pepper. Then add some stock or water and let cook for approximately three-fourths of an hour, add some canned apples or watermelon rind, and some wine. If you've drunk the wine, put in a jigger of vinegar, let simmer five or ten minutes and add a bit of corn starch to thicken. This will give it a nice glaze. Serve it with rice pilaf or steamed rice and if the editor doesn't mind, some stewed egg plant.

Next Thursday, the Lakeshore Merchants Association is having a meeting at my place and I promise to be a good boy. Not like I was at the Grand Ave. Merchants meeting. I'm lucky that they speak to me. I sort of passed out at that meeting, the reason being that I had a flue shot in my right arm, a mercury shot in my left arm and before I came to work I had a knockout pill to quiet my nerves.

Well, sir and mams, with all those drugs, plus three highballs to help me along, everything went sort of blotto for awhile and I remember little if any of what transpired at that meeting. I'm not boasting, I'm properly ashamed, I've been severely chastised for it from sources close to me and it won't happen again. I mean it. I am back in the pink again and ready to greet you all pleasantly the next time I see you. See you next week.

Photo of Fenner with friends in front of the restaurant.

Gourmet Corner

By FENNER FULLER

The reason there wasn't a column last week was, we were flooded out, and how . . . It was quite a lot of fun for awhile, just like dining in Venice. The water was dashing up on the windows with the cars going by making very beautiful waves, in fact they were whitecaps. When the patrons started to leave tho it wasn't so very funny anymore. Men took their shoes and socks off and carried their wives to the cars.

Some of the women were pretty hefty girls too, one man carried his wife out and as he stepped off the curb he fell flat on his .. . .(guess what?). Anyway it was quite a sight. Everyone had a good laugh over it except the man who fell in the water. One customer was quite nervous about a dog he had in his car, so he went out and rescued him and brought him in. I put him in our office while they finished their dinner; however, the dog yelped so much all during dinner I had to turn the music up louder to drown him out.

The next day I came down to clean up and wouldnt' you guess it, it started to rain again. I went in and fixed myself some breakfast and when I came out the water was so high I was trapped. What else was a fellow to do . . . A good restaurant all stocked with fine food and liquor? Naturally I invited in all the neighbors and adjoining merchants and we had a ball. Everything is all cleaned up now and we are thankful we weren't damaged. My heart goes out to those merchants who were damaged and lost business, however it could have been worse so we should be thankful for that.

Here is a good recipe for the Fall days. I'm stealing it from the Virginia City cook book. It's called, "Old Washoe Club Pork Chops." The Old Washoe Club is one of Virginia City's famous thirst quencheries, a-jam with relics of Victorian days and especially proud of tis historic winding staircases. Denny and Mary Copp preside over its various fascinations, and like all Virginia City residents, eat uncommonly well. Mary, with proper modesty, doesnt' call this a recipe, but I think it is an original and a nice idea.

Brown thick pork chops in a skilllet, then for each four pork chops pour on a cup of canned, evaporated milk and simmer until the chops are brown and shiny. Serve on a platter with the sauce poured over the chops. I like the chops served with candied yams and cranberry jelly. Try it, you can add as much salt and pepper as you desire.

Yours for a dry week end, both inside and out.

—Fenner

Photo of Fenner pouring some wine in the restaurant kitchen.

Gourmet Corner
By
Fenner Fuller

This column is so tasteless,(yes even my recipes) its quite child like and I sometimes hesitate to write it however when I skip a week or so I get so many calls asking whats the matter, that I get encouraged and start to writ again. Afrer receiving the big city papers, both Oakland and S.F. I think that the Times is a real newsy local paper, I get so discusted with the big papers it seems that all you get is about six or seven Shopping news put together, just look at them and find something of intrest you wnat to read, you have to go through fifty pages of Blue fronts, Yellow Front store adds and to me it sicking, some of the columest are pretty good but no better that Ben Fong Torres who writes, Funny Side up., read his column, I can't figure if hes a kid, a school boy, married or singel, anyway he is swell, much better than some of the big boys. Then Bill Masterson in "Off the Record", hes a prow. Then there is a girl that workes at Steres Drug Co. she is good also, I can't recall her name, she gives you the local gossip. By the way, have you ever watched channel 9 on T.V. at four thirty Mondays, theres a gal who is a wow at French cooking and she would put you and me to shame, she knows so much and she has so many short cuts to good cooking that it is like shooting fish in a barrel, look at her some time. She isn't fancy and she speaks English and is form Boston I think. Speaking of Frnch cooking try this one."SAUCISSES AU VIN BLANC" (Sausages with white wine) Take as many sausages as you want, butter a pan, put sausages in and sprinkle flour on them, add white wine and place in a moderate oven adding salt and pepper, simmer untill done. just before serving mix in some cream, serve on slices of bread that you have fried in butter to a golden brown, put on a hot plate and serve very hot., please do not ask me what the proportions are I don't know, I do know that you should take a few glasses of wine before you start cooking, this will be an excuse if it doesn't turn out right. I am looking forward to seeing the water turned on in the new fountain on Lake Park Ave. You know if they had turned the water on the kids wouldn't have broken the lights, Oh well, the experts will never learn, why doN't they ask me about thoes things, the boobs., Wouldn't it be nice if they turned the water on and called it a wishing well and let me go over and pick up the money every month, You know what I would do with it, I would black top under the freeway and let the merchants park there all day free, of course for my ida I would take my regular agents cut of 10%. Well dear hearts I will close hoping to see you in the fountain, by the way you can cast in a few dollar bills too if you wish.

                                        Fenner.

Photo of Fenner in his chef's attire.

Gourmet's Corner

I really get a kick out of the big local newspaper and the big ones in San Francisco. Every year they put out a section in their papers called the "gourmet section" and no matter how good the restaurant is they will not mention your name unless you buy a big ad, what a deal. So many folks have asked me why I wasn't mentioned, the reason being I would rather give you a larger portion and a lower price than to pay those buzzards 25 pieces of eight. You know I'm half Scot and I get plenty of free advertising including the plugs I give myself in this column, also being the only restaurant in the Bay Area mentioned in the London Food and Wine Society. I know that doesn't get me much business but perhaps in the future when we get a faster jet from London to our own new Oakland Air Port, business will pick up both for the Port of Oakland and Fenner Fuller's "Hot Dog."

Speaking of hot dogs, try grinding them up and mixing it with ketchup and a bit of mustard. It makes a wonderful sandwich or a spread for crackers, wonderful for cocktail parties. Here's another good cracker deal, grind up raw filet of sole and mix it with chopped black olives, add salt, peper and olive oil. I call it Lake Merritt caviar. A dash of lemon will help. Here is a goodie. "Les Jets De Houblon," that's Belgian for HOP SHOOTS; where in the world could you find Hop Shoots, especially this time of the year, anyway here it is: Boil the shoots in salted water, with a little lemon juice, well drained, and covered with a sauce consisting of a little cream and melted butter, seasoned with salt and pepper. It is put in the middle of a dish, and garnished with poached eggs. O.K., see you in the hop fields.

Photographs of family helping at the restaurant. Top photo is of Fenner's wife, Esther Fuller. Lower left photo is of Fenner's cousin, Eldora. Lower right photo is of Esther's sister, Betty Nielsen.

Gourmet Corner

By FENNER FULLER

Thanksgiving is over and I suppose you have some turkey left over and you might be wondering what to do to get your family to eat leftovers. I will give you a few hints such as chicken Hawaiian or mock turtle soup and no matter how you cook it it is still turkey. But first I want to tell you about my trip to Merced and Turlock. I was invited to help celebrate my cousin's 80th birthday at Merced and I might say I had a ball with all the second and first cousins, some were old and some young. I palled around with the youngsters; they were more fun and seemed to get along better with my jokes. I took four bags of tea to help celebrate and you know what? My cousin Fenner Adolphus Chamberlain wouldn't let me drink any so I went down town and bought a few jugs and hid them in the gaarge, so by taking short walks out in the yard and visiting the garage I managed to have a good time.

Monday and Tuesday I went pheasant hunting with my brother-in-law and I guess I walked all over Merced and Stanislaus county, saw hundreds of birds, and didn't get one. The reason being I had no gun and my sidekick was a bum shot. Anyway, I enjoyed the country. One highlight of the trip was when the game warden stopped us and asked for our license. When he came to my side of the car I opened the window and barked at him like a dog. He said, "What goes?" and I said I was a bird dog. I must say he was frightened and asked me if I had a gun, I said no, and quick like a flash he said, "O.K., wise guy, then let me see your dog license." That's that. It's a good thing I didn't end up in the pound. Now for chicken Hawaiian. Take the turkey meat and heat it up with Lipton's chicken soup base, add green peppers and pimentos, in other words, make creamed chicken, and add a can of pineapple chunks. Serve with rice and top with shredded coconut. No room for the mock turtle soup. Hope to see you soon,

—Fenner Adolphus Chamberlain Fuller.

Undated shot of the front room of the restaurant.

Exterior of the restaurant as of winter 1964.

Front of the restaurant as of Thanksgiving 1964.

Wednesday, February 20, 1963

Gourmet's Corner
By FENNER FULLER

I wrote a column last week and took it up to the Times office and found the door locked (guess they were out selling) and I slipped it under the door, (it was a masterpiece). I had a fond hope that they might find it there when they came in and get it into print. I must have slipped it into a broom closet or something because I never have seen it in the paper although I read it assiduously in the hope that my name will still glitter as brightly as ever after a few tarnishing weeks of lying about in one of the remote recesses of the print shop. Anyway, I'm submiting another one this week for your reading fun and I do hope you enjoy it if you even get to read it.

Today I'm cooking six old hens to get broth for my soup and pilaf and do you know when I tried a piece of one of those old birds it was delicious, too good to cut up for chicken salad, so tonight we are going to have Chicken Friccasee Ala Lucius. Cut chickens up in serving sizes and place in a baking pan. In another pan, add butter, chopped onions, green pepper, mushrooms, pimiento and flour to thicken the butter. In other words make a rue. Add to this the chicken broth and beat with a French whip until smooth, then add some sherry wine and pour over chicken. A very good dish and reasonable.

Reverend Eric Lindholm was in our restaurant the other day and said he enjoyed reading my column. He didn't say much about the food, but he did make me feel good. That's a fine name for him, he is the SHY PILOT over at the Lakeside Baptist Church. Last week they told me he was hoarse and couldn't preach his sermon so they called on my brother-in-law to help him out. Now Reverend, if you had called on me I could have given you a recipe to end all this embarrassment. Cook slowly two onions with some sugar and vinegar. Cook it until it becomes syrupy, then take a spoonful at a time and let it trickle down your throat, it's a sure cure for whatever you had. By the way, this is not recommended by the American Medical Association or the Pure Food and Drug laws, so if it doesn't work, sue me.

I can't find much more to say. Is it possible I'm running out of things to gab about? Why not send me a recipe? I'm serious. Send it in and I'll cook it and try it out and if it suits me I will invite you down for two free dinners on the house. Now don't make it something too difficult, keep it simple, something you think my customers might like. Send your name and address along so I know who to invite. Mail your recipes to The Times at 3410 Lakeshore Ave. See you in the soup,

—Fenner

Photos of Fenner just loafing at his apartment on Merritt Ave in Oakland, CA. Top photo is in the living room, middle shot is in Fenner's bedroom, and the bottom shot is in the backyard as of Sept 1957.

" EVERYBODYS DOING IT "
BY
FENNER FULLER

Just loafing around the house to-day burning up old newspappers and flicking my cigarett ashes at the fire place and missing most of the time, My wife Esther said, what makes you so restless, I dunno, well why don't you do something, what do you want me to do I aaked, she said, go down to the resturant and write a book, just like that, nothing to it Everybodys doing it, so here I am with aFunk and Wagnalls college dictonary, you see I want to be a good writer and not misspell any words, the thing that bothers me is, how you going to look up a word if you cant' spell it, like, does the word start with a ph, or an F, So I8ll just phool around and see what happens.

I could write an autobiography of my self but that would be too easy and besides, I can't tell you about all my secret love afairs, and tell the world what a blister I've been, then again my wife would leave me if she knew all, I just cant be like my friend Henry Miller, I have too many friends that think I'm a right nice guy, and at this late date in my life I don't want to spoil the phony image I have worked so hard to build, so I'll just tell you a few of my thoughts and experancees that have happened that I think you might be intrested in.

Way back in January I3, I902 in the town of Cumberland in the g#rate Stat of Rhode Island I was born. My Mother who was about fourty years old at the time and she had consulted a few country Doctors and they insisted that she had a tumor, well dear hearts, it wasn't a tumor after all, it was me, so now you can say you heard a tumor talking or writing which ever you prefer. They tell me it was so cold that my aunt Hanna put me in a cloths basket and wrapped me in swadling cloths and placed the basket behind the old kitchen stove to keep me from freezing, when the the rest of the household go up for breakfast they heard the crying from behind the stove, in thoes days everybody gathered around the stove to dress, My oldest sister asked papa if one of the cows had calfed during the night, Papa said yes, so why dount you take a look, my sister let out a yell and said with tears in her eyes, What another baby for me to bring up , you see it was the custom in thoes days that the oldest girl had to take care of the babys, me being the sixth, I can see why she was put out. I have a feeling I wasn't wanted, anyway as I grew and could do some chores around the farm, it was then that I became a full fleged member of the clan, everybody worked, thats h#ow Papa beat the labor problem.
As any good write knows, a book has to havechapters, so I'll start another chapter.

51

Photo of Fenner and friend introducing humor at the airport.

Gourmet Corner

By FENNER FULLER

GOURMET CORNER — ST HD

My last column was not the Gourmet Corner, it was inserted next to an ad, which is O.K. by me if you could find it. Anyway I stated that I was getting a bit discouraged because some people informed me that they thought this column was so much "Mish Mash" what ever that is. Anyway I got so many letters asking me to continue, and that my dear hearts gave me a great deal of inspiration, so here I am again. For the past few weeks I have been a bit confused, namely by my not knowing what the right or left is. They talk about the Birchers, and I don't know what they stand for and that bothers me; also St. Patrick's day. Everybody wears green; Oscars on lake shore Ave. gave green hats away to everybody and I hear everybody had a ball, they even had three coppers to keep the bodies in or out, I don't know which. Anyway I guess its O.K. but what bothers me is, Why don't we wear Red White and Blue on Washingtons Birthday, Lincolns birthday, also on the fourth of July. O well, the Irish have a way of selling things even if St. Patrick wasn't Irish and that they had no snakes in Ireland in the first place.

Oh yes, we had corned beef and cabbage on the 17th. That is not an Irish dish, it is Dutch and the Irish picked it up here in the good old U.S.A. I must thank Mrs. R. L. Thompson for her wonderful recipe for leg of lamb creole. I haven't had time to try it, but you can be sure I will. It sounds delish; also Rachael Rasmussen for her delightful "Tipse Chicken". My next column I will write for all the world to know what a wonderful cook you are. Most people don't like peas, please try them this way.

Put a small amount of olive oil in a sauce pan, chop onions into oil and cook onions until golden brown, then add one can of peas and salt and pepper Just heat, that's all. You will love them that way. Potatoes: try this one. 6 medium potatoes, 1-4 cup olive oil, 1 cup tomatoes, 2 tbl. chopped parsley, 1-4 cup diced carrots, 1-4 cup chopped celery, 4 cloves garlic chopped, 2 cups water, 1 tsp. salt, 1-2 tsp. pepper. Slice tomatoes and put into shallow pan. Mix all chopped vegetables together and pour over potatoes. Add the seasoning and water, cover and cook over low fire for one hour.

**Tell Our Advertisers
You Saw It In The Times!**

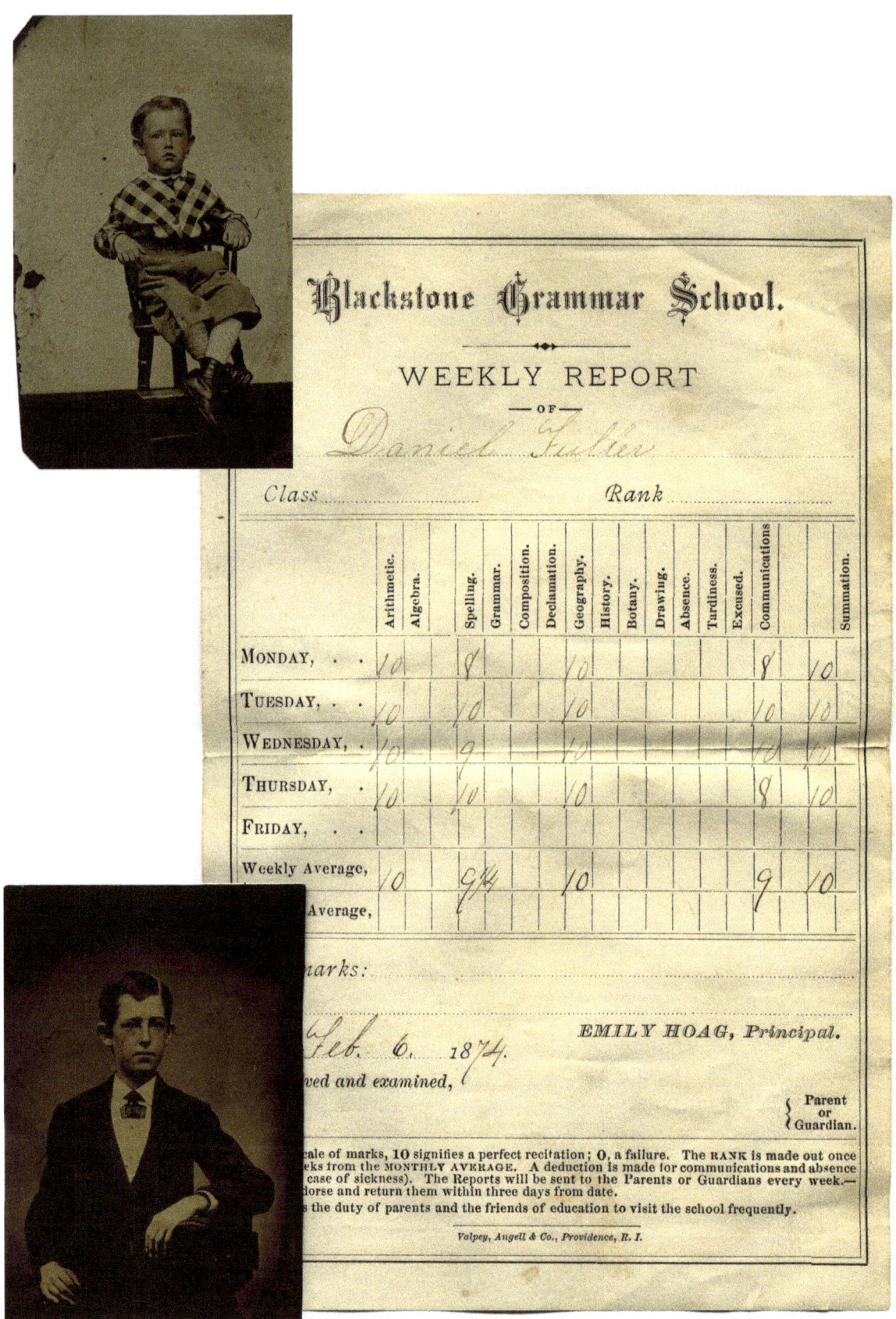

Photos of Fenner's father, Daniel Fuller, along with a weekly report of his grammar school education.

Gourmet Corner

By FENNER FULLER

Easter is here again, and as I recall, it was a very joyous day for us, back in New England. Of course it meant a new suit and shoes; in those days I wore knickerbockers, the coat having a belt, etc. Generally its color was grey and sort of a race track check and believe me, I really looked racey. Anyway, I was a cute coot.

Our family had an early Easter eggs you could eat, a big the egs you could eat, a big slice of ham that Papa had smoked and cured, and johnnycake and gooseberry jam. Mama used to put butter in a large pan, melt it, add rich milk, salt and pepper, drop the eggs into the milk or cream and kind of poach them. Believe me, it was tasty. Try it sometime.

After breakfast, we did all the chores around the farm and then got dressed up for church. Mama, Papa, Leora (my sister), and myself would ride in the surrey with the fringe on top. Gordon and Florita (another brother and sister of mine) would drive the concord buggy and Elmer and Belmont (a couple of other brothers) (what a family we had) would take a four seater wagon, hoping they would snag a couple of girls on the way home.

The church was Christ Episcopal and it was very impressive on Easter Sunday. Stained glass windows with the morning sun shining through on each pew, and Easter lilies that were given away to the shut ins after church. Everyone sang, and they had a wonderful choir. My sister Florita was the soloist and I must say we were all very proud of her.

After services, we would all gather outside and meet all the folks from the town and invariably Papa would invite a crowd up to the farm for dinner which always made Papa happy because it gave him an excuse to try out the hard cider. Of course Mama and my two sisters were not so happy because it threw all the work on their shoulders. Anyway, we fed them Boston baked beans and brown bread, apple pie, coffee and hot chocolate for the kids.

I'm not adding a recipe today because I imagine you have your menu planned for Easter. If you haven't, look through the paper and see my ad, you might be interested in what it offers. A joyous Easter to you all,.

—Fenner

Photo of Fenner with large rabbit he probably constructed himself.

Photo of Fenner in front of the restaurant with a bone mobile. Esther Fuller wrote on the margins that meat was scarce during the war years. So this may have been taken in the mid 40's.

Gourmet Corner

By FENNER FULLER

Oh, what a beautiful Sunday morning this is. At least this is when I wrote this although you will be reading it Wednesday or Thursday. But who cares, everyday is a beautiful day if you can as much as breathe.

Read this one, but don't try it, reason being, I don't think you'd like it. Anyhow, Mr. Paymal of Virginia City who sent it to me must have enjoyed it because he took the trouble to send it to me. He calls is PICKLED or SOUSED tripe. Mr. Paymal said this is a dish that the free loaders got in the old saloons. It was done by boiling the tripe until tender, cutting it into attractive pieces, pouring over them a mixture of two quarts of boiling vinegar, ¼ cup of sugar, two tablespoons of salt, and ¼ cup of mixed pickling spice. Let stand one week before serving.

Pigs feet are soused in the same way. Can't you just hear someone saying, "Come on over to the house for a few cocktails and some soused pigs feet." Sounds revolting.

Yesterday, I told a couple of my patrons I'd like to write a political column, but not knowing where to start thought I'd leave well enough alone. However, I will say I can't see the reasoning of some of the big papers in their recommendations of this or that certain man for position or promotion. Why should they try to twist our thinking around to their way of thinking. Who do they think they are? Anyway we beat City Hall good in this last primary and we'll beat them again in the run offs next month.

Here's another tripe deal; one of Lucky Baldwin's favorites. Cut boiled tripe into long strips, add a number 2½ can of tomatoes, a large onion, sliced, a crushed clove of garlic and a chili pepper with top and seeds removed. Season with salt and simmer for one hour. Thicken the sauce with a roux before serving. I wonder if this is the dish that made Mr. Baldwin lucky?

Everyone in the area is talking about what to do with the space under the new MacArthur Freeway. This is my very own idea; attach old egg crates and boxes of any size to the sides of the bridge and make them into homes for all the homeless pigeons; anything to keep them off the Grand Lake Theater and my awnings. Just think what a grand thing this would be for Oakland, the only city in the world with a million dollar pigeon coop.

See you under the bridge,

—Fenner

46 E Oakland Tribune, Wednesday, Oct. 11, 1950

Going Places

A ROUND GOSSIP

I guess it's been four years now since first I met Big Milt, the smiling boss of Orinda-Willows. That was when we were busy tagging a new name to an old road—"Tunnel Strip."

A lot of martinis have poured down the old hatch since then.

And Milt Nelson is one of the 10 most widely known gents in the Eastbay. Four years ago he was only known to the exclusive little roster of Orinda Country Club members. He was their club manager.

HITS JACKPOT

Some say Milt owes his fame to a ravioli. Others think he just smiled his way to the top. I haven't the least idea what zoomed Moonface Milt to the top rung of the nitery ladder. Point is—he's up there. His spot is making like three bars on a dollar slot machine. That's not the press agent in me a-talking, either. It took his wife, Eve, two days to tally just the Saturday food checks, last week-end.

The rush to Orinda Willows this season is unprecedented. Reason number one: the dinner, a traditional thing of 25 years standing—and Milt is keeping up the two "Q's"—quality and quantity. Number two: Danny Van Allen, a personality you can't help liking—and music to match. Number three: Milt's innovation —the Afternoon Night Club with Lewis and Sanchez making with the rhythm and entertainment.

Just like they say, though—"What's a home without a mother?" What's a nitery without a host? So my little cafe score card gives Milt half the credit, for simply being a jolly, fun-filled host.

Funniest guy I've seen in ages is Woo Woo Stevens, that's his name: "Woo Woo"—and you'll scream, if you're half-way hooman! He's at Bimbo's 365 in SF.

The bombshell coming into Sinaloa, all the way from Mejico, is a temperature raiser, named Yolanda Reyes. Starts Friday, so get your wolf-whistle oiled up.

Tex Wherry is toying with a Texas oil deal that might make him first an Oil Man, secondly the Balalaika boss. Down there now.

Watch for Sophie tonight on KGO-TV, 6:30-7.

Fong Wan would give just about anything, short of the price he has Lana Wong contracted for, to get her back into Club Shanghai. But Lana, she still say "no."

WEDDING EVENT

Rusty Draper's wedding was a cafe society event, Monday night. From the Swedenborgian Church in SF—they went to the Koffee Kup, where Hermie King and his brother, Will, tossed a whale of a reception. The Drapers are honeymooning in NY.

Dates to remember: Marge Knappenberger's fourth anniversary party, that lasts three days, October 18, 19 and 20 (Wednesday through Friday) at El Nido Rancho. She got home from her vacation Monday night. Drove that new Olds about 2000 miles.

The weather has been kind to us at El Nido. Sultry mornings that make our pool terrace broadcast a nice thing on Sundays. We're sold-out-solid week after next—but how's about coming out this Sunday. Meet some of our celebrated guests and get a good half hour of fun and entertainment. Or tune our way— KLX, 11:30-12 a.m.

CREATIVE COUPLE

We spent a full evening at Fenner Fuller's Restaurant last Friday night. Most enjoyable new acquaintances in months. What an exciting couple, these fabulous Fullers, with their creative art ideas, and full circle of appreciative friends! Their restaurant (on Grand) dares be different. A place that appeals to a certain few who recognize food and mood that is far from commercial. Fenner's cooking is something strictly "U..I." He stirs the whole world into a pot and comes up with Food-Fennerisms of many sorts.

Newspaper article showing that evidently sometimes Fenner did get "good press" without having to pay for it.

GOURMET CORNER
BY
FENNER FULLER

5-15-63

Adventures in Good Eating by Duncan Hines, remember him? He put out a Very fine book on where to dine and lodge for the ni g ht, well anyway one of his scouts came to my restaurant in 1945 and wrote a glowing report on Fenner Fullers, I was VERY happy at the good news and thought I would be on my way to fame and fortune, then about six weeks after the report went in I was confronted by a gentleman from Dun can's home office saying I would be mentioned in his then famous book, I cooked him a fine dinner with all the trimmings and everything went along fine untell he asked me to buy two hundred books at a buck per copy, well folks to make a long story short I said, Good by, so I was never mentioned in the famous book A dventures in Good Eating, anyway after nearly twenty years I'm still here. I only mention this beacuse I would like to convey to you that a person can get most anywhere if you pay for it. (Left Over Beef)
MEAT ROLL. Make a regular biscuit dough, roll out to about ½ inch thick. take left over beef (if not ground, grind it), spread over the dough. Sprinkle with chopped onion. Roll like a cinnamon roll and lay in baking dish. If you have some left over gravy pour it over the roll. Bake untill biscuit dough is done and serve as a main dish with vegetables. Be sure the gravy keeps the roll moist. Gosh folks I don8t know what to write about to day, its my day off and I want to pull weeds in my back yard. Kay Masterson wanted me too bevause she is putting out a double header or something. Speaking of weeds, perhaps I should forget my back yard and go over to the park and pull them, on the other hand I like them in in the park, differant. Speaking of the Park, wouldn't you think that His Honer the Mayor would appoint a park commision that knew something about grass and beautiful shrubs and trees, now that Bill Mott## is no longer with the City we are in a fine fix for somebody that knows something about grass, anyway they know how to raise money and weeds.
One of our commisioners should plant " Money Plants"

Fenner

Fenner Fuller's RESTAURANT
CATERING SERVICE — BANQUETS — PARTIES
614 Grand Avenue - Oakland 10, California - Phone HIgate 4-9701

Restaurant logo from cover of wine list and restaurant letterhead.

Wedneseday, May 22, 1963

Gourmet Corner

By FENNER FULLER

Let me think now, what will I write about today? Oh yes, will one of you dear hearts write to the Park Commission and tell them if the weeds are not cut pretty soon we will have a bumper crop next year, the reason being they will turn to seed and will start seeding themselves. Isn't nature wonderful. By the way I read in the Times last week all about the plans for beautifying Lakeshore Ave. It sounds great, but I'll bet the smart boys didn't think of a comfort station or a couple of drinking fountains. Did you know that you can't get a drink of water free on the street or if you have to go you have to ask one of the merchants for a key, by that time it might be too late. Oh well, what the heck, who cares about minor things. It seems to me that the smart boys are getting dumber and the dummies are getting smarter.

Let's see now, what will we cook this week. By the way, did you try the meat roll last week? I did and it was awful, too soggy, so today I'll try and give you a better one. Short ribs of beef: 2 lbs. beef short ribs, 1 clove garlic, 1 small onion, 1 tsp. paprika, salt, pepper, 2 or 3 cloves, 1 cup catsup. Have short ribs cut into pieces suitable for servings. Rub with cut garlic, roll in seasoned flour. Brown on all sides in hot fat. Sprinkle with salt and pepper and slice onion over top. Half cover with boiling water. Cover pan closely and simmer for about 2 hrs. Add catsup, cloves and water if necessary. Continue simmering until tender.

By the way, a great many of you readers of the Times came to our dining room on Mother's Day and mentioned this column and I want to thank you for coming and building up my ego. Both Mrs. Fuller and I want to thank you and we do hope you enjoyed yourself.

See you at the comfort station or the water fountain.

—Fenner

Photos of Robert and Lydia Court and their children. Robert was a violinist with the Paganini Quartet. Their first meals after they arrived from Belgium were at the restaurant.

GOURMET CORNER
BY
FENNER FULLER

6-5-63

Through this column I wish to thank Mrs. Ziegenfuss and her party for coming in and having dinner, she is a very jolly girl and most of her party said they enjoy my column but enjoyed the dinner better. Mrs. Ziegenfuss when she called tom make a reservation joked about her name and informed me that the name ment in German, (Goats Foot) and laughed about it. I love thoes kind of names like Gerstenfeld which means Corn field. Speaking of Goats Feet I must give you a favorate receipe for, get this now, hold your hats,(KOUZOU KZARTMA) thats as close as I can get to goat feet, its Lamb Shanks. 4 shanks of lamb. 4 large potatoes 2 tomatoes quartered, 2 teaspoonfulls salt, I teaspoon paprika, 2 cups water. Wash lamb well and let stand in clean water for at least I5 minutes. Place in open roasting pan; add tomatoes, salt, paperika, and water. Cook for half hour at 375 deg., turn meat over and cook another half hour. Now add potatoes and roast with the shanks for 30 minutes, then turn both potatoes and meat and let cook for another thirty min. Meat should cook for two hours altogether. serve with its own juice as gravy. Good served with pilaff. If you want to be a bit crazy like I am add some tomato puree and some sherry wine, gives it a bit of a lift. Every columnist on this paper, which I think is The newesy sheet in town,(dear hearts its all truth.) What I started to say, Bill Masterson (off the record) and Wally White seemed to be apologies to everyone. Fellows never do that, when we write it comes out of great minds and at the time we ment it, so dond't go back on what you say. If we dont say the right thing AT the right time there is really something wrong with us. so untill next week, I'll be seeing you in the (Goat Shed)

Fenner.

Put this one in first.

George Mardikian Services

Funeral services will be held in San Francisco this evening for celebrated restaurateur George Magar Mardikian, who died at his Pacific Heights home Sunday while recovering from a heart attack suffered last May. He was 73.

Mr. Mardikian came to the United States from his native Armenia in 1922 and parlayed a hearty appetite and a zest for good cooking into the well-known Omar Khayyam's Restaurant at 196 O'Farrell street.

He became a friend of presidents and generals and toured the world's battlefronts from 1942 to 1954 as food consultant to the United States Army.

He liked to tell army mess sergeants that they were competing with every soldier's mother and that they had better use their wits to convert a slice of Spam into something more appetizing and attractive.

Mr. Mardikian began his career in the U.S. as a busboy and dishwasher but rapidly became a chef and opened his first Omar Khayyam's in Fresno in 1930.

That restaurant became an immediate success. Eight years later, Mr. Mardikian bought Coffee Dan's at O'Farrell and Powell streets, where he had earlier worked as dishwasher, and opened Omar Khayyam's of San Francisco.

Mr. Mardikian was a founder of the American National Committee to Aid Homeless Armenians and an enthusiastic supporter of the Boy Scouts.

He was a 1951 recipient of the Medal of Freedom (the nation's highest civilian award) for his services to the armed forces.

He was also honored last April as one of six prominent U.S. immi-

GEORGE MARDIKIAN
Friend of presidents

grants at the official opening of Ellis Island as a national historic site.

Mr. Mardikian was the author of two books—"Song of America,"
an autobiographical account of his rise to success, and a cookbook, "Dinner at Omar Khayyam's."

Mr. Mardikian's wife of 47 years, Nazenig, died in August from lung cancer.

He is survived by a daughter, sculptress AnitaNaz Mardikian; a son, Haig Mardikian; and one granddaughter, Sasha Lund Mardikian.

Funeral services will be held at 6:30 p.m. this evening (Tuesday) at Halsted and Co. Mortuary, 1123 Sutter street.

Wednesday, funeral services will be held again at 1 p.m. at the Holy Trinity Armenian Apostolic Church, at Ventura and M streets in Fresno. Interment will be at the Armenian Ararat Cemetery in Fresno.

The family has asked that contributions be made to the Western Prelacy of the Armenian Apostolic Church of America for distribution in Mr. Mardikian's memory to Armenian schools in San Francisco and Los Angeles.

Tribute to George Mardikian in the Oct 25, 1977 edition of the SF Chronicle, describing George's full life. Photo of Fenner and George on the deck of Fenner and Esther's apartment

GOURMET CORNER
BY
FENNER FULLER

7-17-63

As you perhaps know, I didn't write a column last week, the reason being, I wrote a long letter to my friend George Mardikian who has had a heart attack in Allentown Penn. I called him up the other day and he is walking around his room, I told him all about Our Liberty Bell that was hidden in Allentown during the Revolution, as if he didn't know, I told him to look under the bead and he might find another relic, who knows, Allentown is an old town. Mrs. Mardikain asked me to write to him often as he got a big kick out of my crazy letters, so it has keept me very busy thinking up stories that might give him a chuckel. I can't write all I want to because his dear wife reads them too, and that would get back to my wife and that wouldn't be so good. You know George who owns OmarKhayyam's Rest. in San Francisco, He's the guy that taught me the business and that is why my Armenian food has a Scotch accent. Last week My wife and I went over to Carmel for a few days, I went for a rest but didn't get it because we had to trapes through all the art shops, and believe you me that is no rest for me, anyway it made her happy. I wanted to get a good fish dinner on the wharf at Monterey and we really got rooked, We want into one of thoes fish places recomended by the California Auto Association thinking that that firm should know their business. Now I want to know what a club like the A.A.A. knows about food, roads, Gasoline and oil, but food no. Just because a restaurant has stainless steel ranges and bright lights don't make the food good, if you know anybody that works for the A.A.A. tell them to get out of the recomending where to eat, and stick to the road maps. Gosh I havent much room left on this sheet to give you one of my masterpieces but I asure that next week will be better. Anyway I don't think you want to cook in the hot weather so, why not come to my place and leave the dishes to us.

See you under the bed in Allentown.
Fenner

Photos of Fenner extolling the wonders of fresh produce at the Mardikian ranch.

Wednesday, July 24, 1963

Gourmet Corner

By FENNER FULLER

Before I give you my masterpiece recipe today I must write about the restaurants that have taken up counterfeiting, I can see why the masterminds of the ring picked the restaurant men to do the job of selling the bogus bills. First off, most eating places are counterfeiting something every day, like instant potatoes, instant coffee, instant soups, and of course tenderized steaks, so you can see the restaurant men are used to things like that and it doesn't bother them a bit.

If they would only have come to me first I could have told them they haven't got a chance to get by making money. When I was a kid back in Massachusetts I used to be an engraver of jewelry and the man that worked at the next bench to me told me that when he was younger he engraved on a copper plate a one dollar bill. He wanted to get a job at the mint in Washington, D. C. and took this plate along to show the mint boys a sample of his work. They looked it over and printed a few bucks, they then destroyed the copper plate and told my man in question that they didn't need any engravers. However, for the rest of my co-worker's life the treasury boys were on his tail and every month of his life they would investigate his home and where he worked and what he was doing in his spare time.

So, you see, if you are a good engraver you are followed all your life. Now dear, hearts, if they had of asked me, I would have told them to counterfeit Blue Chip stamps, they are easy to get rid of. A person might not make a million but it would be an easy living.

From India, Mint chutney: ¼ lb. of fresh mint, 1 small onion, lemon juice, black and red pepper, salt. Pound the mint and chopped onion in a mortar, season with salt and pepper, and moisten with the lemon juice. It should be thick and smooth paste. I don't know what you would use it on, perhaps Bombay Duck. Bombay Duck is not a duck. It's some kind of fish caught in the Persian Gulf and when it is cooked it smells awful, so perhaps you can use the chutney after all.

See you in the school printing shop!

Photos of Fenner playing and working hard at the Mardikian ranch.

Gourmet Corner

By FENNER FULLER

I sure goofed last week. Reason being, George Mardikian invited me up to his ranch in St. Helena where he is recovering from a recent heart attack and I am here ostensibly to keep him company. I got here to to find that he is taking good care of himself and looks better than I do. The reason he looks so good is because he is sticking to a diet of 1,000 calories per day but he gets a kick out of cooking for me and watching me eat. He makes me eat all

the things he likes for himself. They say cowboys like to die with their boots on, but not me, I will probably pass on with a full stomach.

Speaking of food, George just told me of a recipe he thought you folks might enjoy. Hold on to your hats, this recipe is for 4 people. Here it is: Take 1 lb. lamb stew meat, braise well in a covered pan for about 5 minutes, use no oil or fat, there is enough fat in the meat. Then add 1 large chopped onion to meat and braise for another 5 minutes. Add 1 cup solid pack tomatoes to onions and meat, juice and all, 2 cans of French cut string beans (with juice), salt and pepper, 2 cups of water, and cook for 1 hour over slow fire with cover on the pan.

George tells me it will serve 4, I say it looks more like 6 can get plenty from it. You have to have French bread to soak up the broth (just dunk it.) It's good, I've had it for 3 straight meals and I'm not tired of it yet. For an added touch to serve on the side with this dish, MISSOV LOBIA, that's what the string bean stew is called. Serve it with sliced cucumbers mixed with yogurt.

I sincerely hope I'm not boring you with so much about Mr. Mardikian, but he is a most interesting character, he owns and operates Omar Khayyam's restaurant in San Francisco, has written several books and is well known throughout the United States. I asked him how he could be so jovial and happy after such a serious heart attack and he replied that he was so happy because it had happened in Allentown, Pennsylvania.

When I asked why, he said that in Allentown he had no friends or relatives. If he had suffered the attack here on the coast where he lives, he would have been swamped with relatives and phone calls from long faced friends, which would have depressed him, and possibly resulted in fatal consequences. So he thanks God that it happened 3,000 miles away where he was assured rest and quiet until he was recovered sufficiently to return home. Does this make sense to you? It does to me. Moral: If you get sick, keep your friends and relatives at home and get well with the help of God, the doctor, nurses and your own efforts.

It's very enjoyable here on the ranch. I'm writing this column under a tree that I planted myself 20 years ago and it must be at least eight feet in circumference today and about 50 feet tall. Yesterday I disced up 20 acres of land to get it ready for alfalfa. I really get a kick out of hard work. There is something great about handling a powerful tractor, I can't explain it to you, but it does something for me. You should have seen me after I finished this project, I was dust from top to bottom. The only white thing visible was my pearly teeth. I didn't want to dirty up the bath room so I went down and jumped into the river to get most of the dirt off.

I didn't bother to undress just jumped in clothes and all I might add that I was cold sober if you have any doubts as to the state of my sobriety. The clothes needed it as much as I did.

Anyhow, I'll see you next week, I'll be cleaned up and smelling like a rose. If any of what you're thinking, I asked the same question. Ice Follies inside of the Claremont Hotel?

It seems they have a portable ice rink that they set up

Photo of Republican convention in San Francisco which George Mardikian catered with Fenner's help.

Gourmet Corner

By FENNER FULLER

Gee whiz, What will I write about today? Oh, I know. Last week I sneaked up to St. Helena to visit my friend George Mardikian, you remember I wrote about him a week or so ago. He is recuperating from a heart attack so I thought it was about time I should give him some "Heart therapy". This is the way I did it. We took a long walk over the ranch "up hill..... Everything was fine with him but my old ticker was pounding like a trip hammer. The next treatment was a short ride in his speed boat. We started off very slow to get him used to the movement of the boat, then I gave the motor full speed ahead and made a few circles around the lake then three or four figure eights, criss crossing the wake of the boat which gave us quite a bouncing and soaking. then coming up to the dock at about twenty knots and missing the dock by inches, I turned my head around to George and said "Great therapy, hey Geo." After we made a landing he looked at me and said, "Fenner? your a sadist, but I feel great, really folks I think he is cured. So if any of you readers have any heart ailment just call Dr. Fenner Adolphus Chanberlain Fuller and I will give you the full treatment. By the way, I also have a distant relative that is in the undertaking business.

While at ranch George gave me a dish of prunes and they were delicious, I asked how he cooked them and he said, come out in the kitchen and I'll show you, You know what? he didn't cook them at all, he just washed them and soaked them in cold water and let them soak over night, I thought that was quite a deal and he told me, why cook them when the sun has cooked them for you. Try prunes St. Helena you will love them. There are times that I get tired of writing about cooking because I have so many other things to write about but I guess I'll have to leave the other things to the experts. No matter how many recipes I give you it will not do you any good unless you have the main ingredient whish is, (quote from George) "LOVE OF COOKING" so, if you don't love cooking, come down to my place and leave the dishes to us. See you in my Heart Therapy class.

Fenner

Photos of Fenner making and displaying his ceramic clowns. The bottom photo was taken shortly after the restaurant opened in 1947-48.

Wednesday, August 21, 1963

Gourmet Corner

By FENNER FULLER

Here we go again, my desk is piled high with bills to be paid and I haven't enough dough to pay them so the heck with them, let them wait awhile longer. It seems that all during the month of July and August I have paid taxes, taxes, taxes, that's the reason for the delay. I guess I'll have to go into the bogus money deal with the rest of the boys. Anybody know of a good school that has a printing press in the basement?

Last Sunday we had old fashioned pot roast and for a change I cooked potato pan cakes and this is the way I fixed them. Grate as many potatoes as you want, (raw) add just a pinch of salt and pepper and very small amount of flour, some chopped parsley and as many eggs as you think you should use to hold the potatoes together, spoon onto a well greased grill or a heavy frying pan. They cook in about five minutes. Don't use too much grease or oil. Very good.

Any of you dear hearts like my idea about the parking garage under Lake Merritt? If so write to your congressman and get him to put the loan through, Oakland should get some of that pork that Washington is handing out, (note) if you are a Republican don't write, you won't stand a chance. Ask one of your Democrat friends to do the dirty work. Now if you will just wait a second, I want to paw through some of these bills and make sure I don't go to jail. on the other hand I have an idea that I would have a lot of fun in jail. They tell me McNeil Island is a wonderful vacation spot, I could teach the other cons how to make clowns or I could cook the Sunday dinner for the guards, there are many things I could do that I think the boys would like, I might even come out with a new trade such as making bogus money, they say its a good place to learn those things. No, there are now pressing bills. I put them out of my sight and I feel better. Whenever you are depressed with bills, just hide them and you will feel better right away. Now my dear hearts if you feel sorry for me come on down to the restaurant and spend a buck or two. If you don't eat I'll have a wishing well installed in the lobby, that's a good racket, isn't it?

Well, I'll see you in the cell block.

Fenner

Photo of Fenner adoring his look-alike clown bust taken on the birthday of Fenner's wife, Esther, Nov 5, 1962

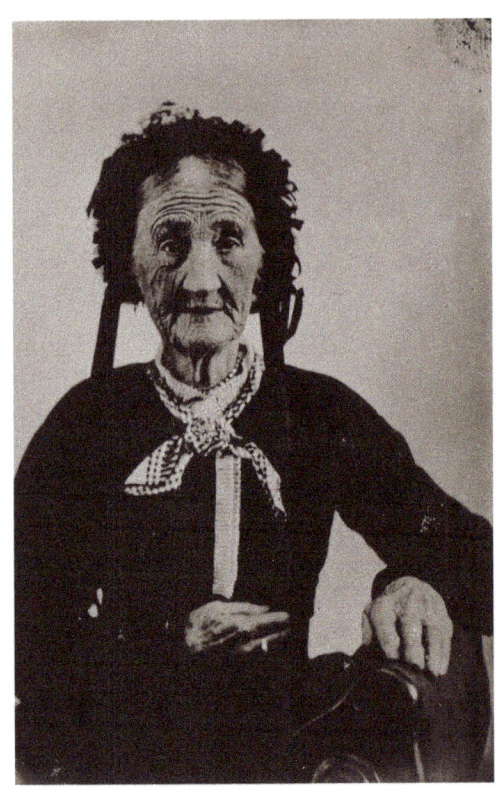

Sally A. Patt, Fenner's grandmother.

Elijah Baker Fuller, Fenner's grandfather(1829-1912). Photo taken in or near Pawtucket, RI.

Fenner Fuller

Fenner's parents, Daniel and Margaret Fuller, taken in Rhode Island, 1888.

Gourmet Corner

By FENNER FULLER

Labor Day, boy what a day that was for the Fuller's back on the farm in R.I.; This was in the 1906 to 1910 era. Papa and the boys would hitch up two rigs, the family surrey with the purple fringe on top, and the old covered milk wagon. I used to ride in the milk wagon and, believe me, it was a great thrill because I couldn't see out, it was fun to try and guess where we were. Every once in a while I would stand up and look out the window in the rear and marvel at how far we had come (perhaps two miles) or so, gosh that was a long way for a six year old.

We were to gather at The Chapel Four Corners for a picnic and clam bake. Boy, was that something in my young life, never did I see such a large crowd, (maybe fifty) anyway it was more that I could count at that time. American flags all over the place, one flag in particular was one that was at Bunker Hill and there were bullet holes in it (so the old guy said).

Paper lanterns strung all over the place, lemonade, cakes, candy, and of course the men had hard cider statched out in the carriage house, it was a wonderful excuse for the men to say to their wives, "Dear I have to go out to the shed and see how the horses are. It worked too. I remember the large band stand covered with bunting, perhaps it was eight feet square. It looked large to me. On the stand the Bell family entertained us, violin organ and a squeeze box, what a combination. Anyway, I marveled at their skill. After dark, different groups would get together and sing. Of course, the (cider boys) were the best. For the climax Magic lantern slides were shown, beautiful pictures, and what a laugh we got when one or two slides were shown up side down. About this time I was put to bed in the milk wagon with a patch work quilt over me, what happened after that I don't know. Oh, I forgot you must have a recipe or they will not call this column a gourmet corner. How about SUCCOTASH New England style. 2 cups cooked lima beans, 2 cups cooked corn, 4 tablespoons butter, ½ cup of rich milk, salt and pepper to taste. Lightly mix vegetables in double boiler, add butter and milk, put over boiling water and heat. See you in the milk wagon.

Photos of Lake Merritt (Oakland, CA) taken from Fenner's apartment on Merritt Ave.

GOURMET CORNER
BY
FENNER FULLER

9/25/63 ISSUE

Last night a Doctor was in and mentioned my column, he said he quit reading it because I skipped around too much and it didn't make sense, well folks that makes a lot of thinking for me, its reasonable because I started off as a Presbyterian, later went to the Methodest, Babtis, Episcopal, Lutherian, Unitarian, Cathloc, Congreational, Seventh Day Adventis, Oh yes, The Assembly of God and a host of other Churches and I haven't been straightened out yet, so how in the world does the dear Dr. expect me to write. By the way the Dr. in question is a dentist, he is a (Orthodontia) hes the guy that corrects the faulty position of the teeth, do you suppose he could help me? perhaps put a brace on my muddled mind. If the Dr. was a student of the future he would read me every week, I guess he didn't know that I have planned to drain Lake Merritt and put a parking lot under the lake or about paving the underpass at Grand and Lakeshore Aves, for parking, or narrowing the side walks on both avenues and parking in the middel of the street and putting a uniform marque all along the sidewalks so we could shop in comfort in the rainy season, also the comfort stations, come come now Dr., lets get hep. (Thin Indian Bread) from the Narragansett tribe. 2 cups water-ground corn meal, I tablespoon butter, I tsp. of salt, boiling water, I cup cold milk, 2 eggs well beaten. Mix together corn meal, buttery and salt, Scald with boiling water to a consistency of thick mush. Mix well. thin down with cold milk and eggs. spread thin on a buttered baking pan. bake untill brown in a moderate oven (350). serve hot. I don't think the Indians used butter, perhaps they used bear or goose grease,(blah). Now lets see what will come out of my Hop,skip and a jump mind Doctor? Oh yes, you might be intrested in this, when I was a kid my second teeth came out in a double row, this is what I did, I put a string on my two baby teeth next to the double teeth and pulled them out myself, then I preceeded to rub my gums, and in about two years my teeth were straightened, no unsightly braces and the cost was nothing. So my young readers if you have and (Orthodontia) trouble come and see Dr. Quack Painless Fuller, no charge, just buy a dinner if you have any teeth.
So long, Painless Fuller.

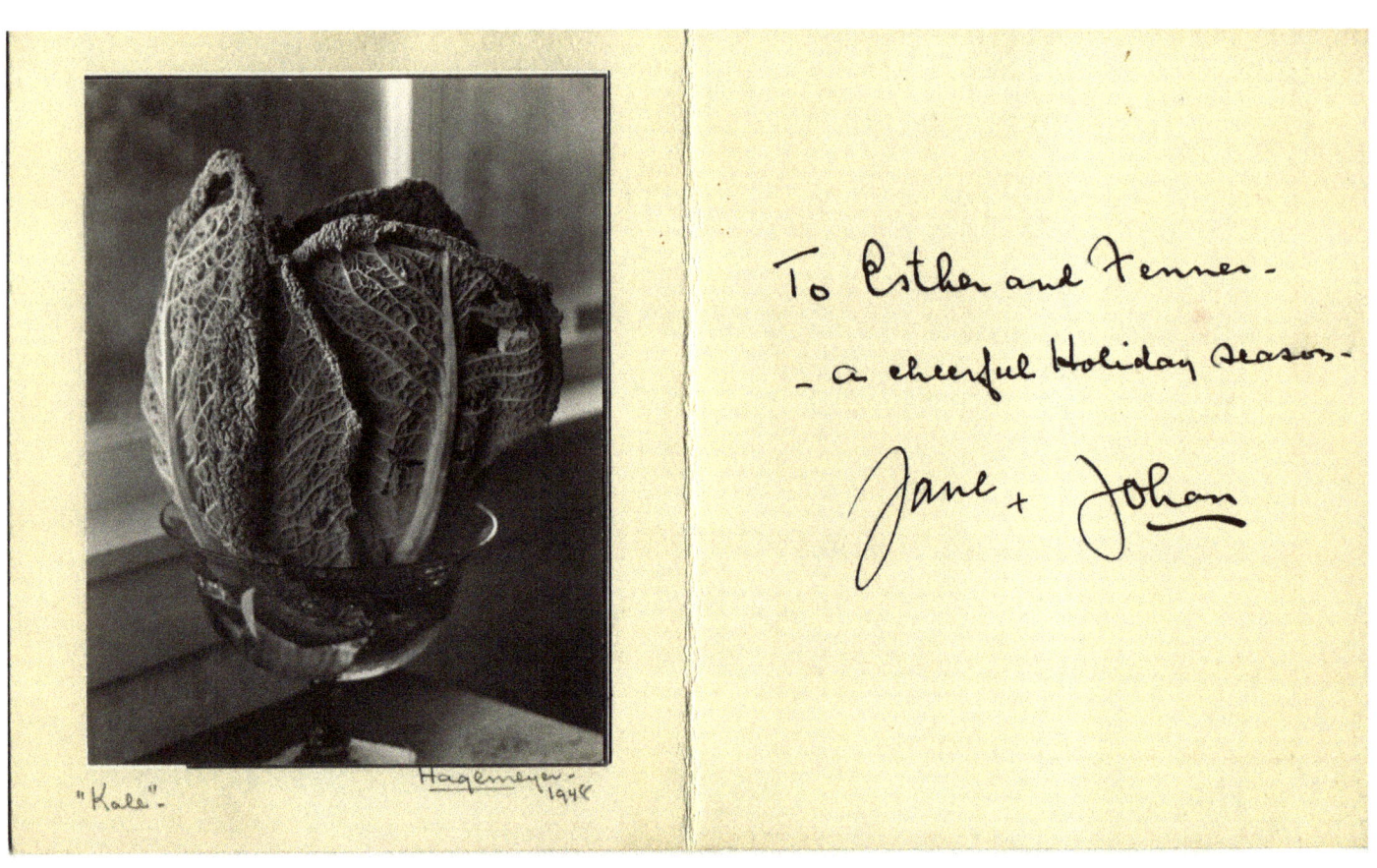

Christmas card from famous photographer Johan Hagemeyer
who took some portrait
photographs of Esther (Fenner's wife) in 1946 and ate at the restaurant.

Wednesday, October 9, 1963

Gourmet Corner

By FENNER FULLER

Well, the three wheeler did it to me again.

I found myself without parking meter change, so I dashed into the restaurant and got a handful of change. When I came out this "vinegar puss" cop was right in back of my car reaching for his book and I said, "Officer;" he just didn't look at me, started writing out the ticket, so I threw the change at him and came back in the place and took a double shot to cool me off.

Boy, oh boy, where in the heck does the police department find these guys with ice water in their veins instead of blood?

It makes me think of a story of a member of a minority group who was driving from the north to the south. The coppers arrested him for going twenty-seven miles an hour in a twenty-five mile zone, they left him in jail for five days and when he came to trial the judge said, "Are you guilty?", and the man said "Yes."

"O.K., said the judge, "That will be five thousand dollars."

"Where in the heck will I get five thousand dollars?", asked the victim.

"Well," said the judge, "Boy, you just take a look out that window. See that bullldog down there. Well that dog is the most vicious dog in the whole south. If you can whip that dog, you can go scot free. The poor guy had no choice so the two coppers took him out in the back yard where the dog was tied up, then they tied the victims hands behind his back and if that was not enough, they dug a big hole in the ground just deep enough for the poor guy's head to stick out.

They let the dog loose and the dog ran around and made a couple of passes at this boy and the poor fellow didn't know what to do. Anyway, he took a bite at that dog and got hold of his ear and really clamped down hard and the dog yelped and yelped and he had him about subdued when the vinegar blooded coppers came up to the poor boy and started kicking him in the head and said:

"Fight fair, boy, fight fair."

Why we don't have pretty young girls doing this job, I don't know. You should see the beautiful girls in Tracy and Gilroy and a few other towns in California. A person doesn't mind getting a ticket if you get a sweet smile along with it.

I can't think of a thing to cook today with the possible exception of how to cook a three-wheeler.

First I would stuff him with old parking tickets seasoned with used crankcase oil, smear with cup grease and slip him in a good sized truck inner tube and cook in the sun, then ship him to the Braziilan jungle. They would find it good eating. So long, see you at dinner.

—Fenner

Fenner fishing and cleaning fish caught at the Mardikian ranch.

Wednesday, October 23, 1963

Gourmet Corner

By FENNER FULLER

"Hi, there, Harry, where are you going?"

"I'm rusing down to Luke's to get a bucket of suds for the old man."

That's one way of expressing it or he might have said that he was rushing the "Growler." In other words, he was going down to the bar to get a pail of beer for his father and perhaps his mother had a hand in it too.

He would enter the side door of the bar which was called the "family entrance." It was a small room directly in back of the bar where the old blisters of the town would go in and have a few horns. In my younger days women were not allowed into drinking places with the men.

I still think it's a good idea. Most of the men that worked in the cotton mills would have their kids carry their lunch buckets down to them. This bucket had four compartments in it. They were used for stews, spuds, bread, and tea or coffee. It was a very useful bucket, being used on occasion for lunches, "suds," and picking huckleberries on Saturday. I often wonder where a fellow could buy a dinner bucket like that today. Also lamp wicks and penny clay pipes. Then there were the old fashioned kerosene cans. Nobody ever invented a better stopper for the kerosene can than the potato. Remember? If I'm writing about things that seem over your head, perhaps we should talk about gas jets and the up to date mantle. What was the mantle made of and why didn't it disintegrate when you lit it? I know it was made of silk, but what made it stay together?

Getting back to potatoes, Yesterday I cooked, so I must tell you what I made that was outstanding. I grated some raw potatoes mixed with some crab meat, added eggs, salt and pepper, and mixed it all together in a light batter and formed "patties." I then grilled sliced tomatoes dipped in a light egg batter. It went over very well. You should try it sometime.

Last week I went up to George Mardikian's ranch but didn't do very much because it rained all day Tuesday and I got tired of hanging around the house listening to Armenian music so I said to George, "I'm going fishing, want to come along?"

"In this rain? Are you nuts?"

"Yes," I said, and I went out to the shed and found a big umbrella that is supposed to go on a tractor.

Well, Sir, I really looked funny holding his big tent over my head and casting with my other hand but I caught four of the nicest bass that were ever caught there. So long, see you under the bumbershoot.

—Fenner.

Signed program from exhibition of four artists who exhibited at the restaurant in 1946. Front and back covers to the right. Inside of program below.

JOHN STOLL
WILLIAM HESTHAL
EDWARD HAGEDORN
BENIAMINO BUFANO

PRESENTED BY FENNER and ESTHER FULLER
614 GRAND AVE., OAKLAND, APRIL 25, 1946

THIS EXHIBITION IS MAKING HISTORY ≡ FOR THE FIRST TIME AN EXHIBITION IS BEING ARRANGED IN WHICH THE INDIVIDUAL ARTIST RECEIVES COMPENSATION ≡ THIS MARKS A NEW DEPARTURE WHEREIN THE ARTIST ≡ THE GALLERY ≡ AND YOU THE PEOPLE COOPERATE TO BRING THE WORK OF THE ARTIST TO THE PEOPLE WHO THUS ARE GIVING AN OPPORTUNITY TO APPRECIATE AND ENJOY ART ≡ THIS IS DEMOCRACY AT WORK ≡ "THAT WE INVITE ARTISTS OF THE BAY AREA AND IF POSSIBLE OF ALL THE STATE OF CALIFORNIA ≡ THAT THE ART COMMISSION PAY THE ARTISTS THE MINIMUM SUM OF TEN DOLLARS $10 FOR EACH ENTRY ≡ THE ARTISTS HAVE ALWAYS BEEN SILENT SO TO SPEAK OF ANY PAY OR COMPENSATION FOR THEIR WORK ≡ WE KNOW THAT IN MUSEUMS AND ART GALLERIES PAY IS RECEIVED BY ALL EMPLOYEES FROM THE ELEVATOR BOY TO THE CURATOR ≡ AND NONE OF THESE EMPLOYEES HAS EVER BEEN KNOWN TO WORK FOR NOTHING ≡ THE ARTIST WHO ALONE IS RESPONSIBLE FOR THE MAINTENANCE OF ALL EMPLOYEES' JOBS RECEIVES NO COMPENSATION AND MORE THAN OFTEN HAS TO TAKE THE RESPONSIBILITY IN THE LOSS OF HIS WORK ≡ AND WHAT IS MORE UNJUST HE MUST PAY FOR SENDING HIS WORK TO AND FROM THE MUSEUM ≡ THIS UNJUST AND UNDEMOCRATIC PRACTICE SHOULD BE ABOLISHED ≡ ART IS THE PEOPLE'S ONE WORLD ≡ ONE COLOR ONE RACE ≡ IT IS THE ONLY UNIVERSAL LANGUAGE SPOKEN ≡ CHERISHED AND UNDERSTOOD BY EVERY PEOPLE OR RACE ON EARTH IT IS THE BASIC ALPHABET OF HUMAN COMMUNICATION" ≡ BENIAMINO BUFANO QUOTATION FROM THE THREE POINT PROGRAM OF THE SAN FRANCISCO ART COMMISSION

Gourmet Corner

By FENNER FULLER

Guess what?

I was invited to the San Francisco Wine Fair last Sunday to demonstrate my famous recipe for cooking oysters and smoked kippers in wine.

I was very pleased to note that I was the only "Chef" from tht Eastbay that was invited. (I Love Me). Incidentally, there were some fine Chefs there. Chef Paola Bermani of Doros, Andre Jouanjos of Alexis, Tangier; Walter Frey of the Sheraton Palace and others.

You should have had an opportunity to taste some of the dishes they prepared. There were strips of bas, dipped in soy sauce and white wine, and then boiled in another kind of wine for about three minutes. Really, it was raw, and it made me gag, guess I'm not a raw fish gourmet. However, the spectators ate it and seemed to enjoy it, perhaps it was because it was free and they were half crocked on the wine they'd been imbibing. The wine was furnished free of charge by the several wineries represented at the Wine Fair.

By the way, I might as well tell you how I prepared the kippers. Unless you are a real epicurean, you won't like this. If you'd like to try it for kicks, here it is:

One can of Cross and Blackwell smoked kippered herring. Place kippers in a well buttered frying pan, not too hot but just hot enough to melt the butter. Cover and add sherry wine and let it sort of steam. When fish is hot, remove with a spat onto a warm platter. Then fry two eggs in the sherry and butter. Sprinkle with sweet basel, put cover back on pan so the eggs will steam and cook on top. Then place the eggs on top of the kippers. I like this, let me know how you make out.

I don't know how you folks are getting along but everybody says that things are getting tough all over. I mean moneywise. They all have a different theory, but I know the real reason and I'll be happy to tell you. Our Government has given away in foreign aid since 1946, 148½ bilion dollars. That's more than the assessed valuation of all the property (including land) in the 50 largest cities in the U.S. It all started back in 1944 in New Hampshire "Breton Woods" when Mr. Harry Dexter White was assistant United States Treasurer. He was also a member of the Council on Foreign Relations and was doing the strongarm work for F.D.R. and Henry Morgenthau. He had them both right by the nose. Later they found out that Mr. White was an undercover espionage agent for the Soviet Union.

See you in Potters field.

—Fenner

Photo of Fenner and Esther listening to an explanation from Bufano of artwork displayed in the back room of the restaurant.

Wednesday, November 13, 1963

Gourmet Corner

By FENNER FULLER

The publisher of this paper who writes the column "Off the Record" is probably going to be real sore at me for writing this column. He said in his Nov. 6th column that the Lake area is sadly lacking in establishments that cater to the needs of the true gourmet.

What the heck does he think my place is? He went on to say about a small but cute place up the avenue that was going to start serving sea foods along with their regular menu, that this might be the answer to what the area needed. Well, I'll bet it will be French fried filet of sole and all the other frozen jazz that is on the market.

He makes me think of those Automobie Clubs that run a towing service and print road maps who take it upon themselves to recommend fine places to eat as tho they knew all about good food. Our big city daily recently put out a Gourmet Guide. For your information they will list anybody that has the price ti pay for the ad. Look the sheet over. Do you thinnk that a man who stands up at a hot dog counter and eats a hot dog wrapped in a paper napkin is a gourmet? Come on now my good friend and publisher, you know that your old Uncle Fenner is the only restaurant recomended by the London Food and Wine Society, the San Francisco Wine Society and the Berkeley Club...

Oh well, I'll let it drop because after he reads this I might get canned as a columnist and you will have to forego your favorite food specialist. I am merely writing this to let him know he should not stoop to write anything for the sake of a fifteen dollar ad. Let the Oakland Times be a "free" press, Bill.

Well, here it is Thanksgiving again and I have just finished reading a recipe in an old 'Army' cook book. No. C-16. The recipe is for Cranberry Relish. It will make one hundred servings.

Make ¼ cup each of 7 oranges and 3 lemons. Wash oranges and lemons, remove peel and quarter. Remove seeds, grind, and/or chop fine. Wash three and a half pounds or three and one half quarts of cranberries. Use four pounds or 2½ quarts of sugar. Combine the fruit and berries, add sugar and mix well. Refrigerate for a few hours before serving. I'm going to serve it with our Thanksgiving dinner which will be a wow cooked by a New Englander. Now don't you think it might be fun to reduce the portion down from a hundred to about eight or ten for your own family? If you get stuck with the figures, you might call the IBM Co. Well, so long for now, see you at the hot dog stand for Thanksgiving, Bill. Perhaps if we have a drink or two, we can eat the soggy napkin.

—Fenner

Armenian friends. Richard Hagopian (top) was an author and Lucine Amara (bottom) was an opera singer. Both enjoyed eating at the restaurant.

Gourmet Corner

By FENNER FULLER

Yep, Thanksgiving is close at hand because some of the merchants have their Christmas decorations up already. This seems stupid to me. I don't think they know what the score is. Most folks laugh at them and I think it looks a bit greedy for business. However a customer was in last night who owns a dress shop in East Oakland and I asked her if she had their fall dresses in the window and she looked at me in dismay and said, heck Fenner we are showing spring dresses. Well I guess I'm the dope.

Last week a customer brought me a wild goose to cook for he and his party. After patching up a broken wing and leg and removing twenty six buck shot, it was ready to cook. I made a stuffing of bread, grapes and apples, rubbed butter on it and wrapped it in foil and roasted it in a slow oven for two hours. I decorated it so it looked like a magazine ad and then took it into the kitchen and carved it. You know what, it was as dry as stale ginger bread. However I made a nice sauce with red currant jelly and orange juice and it wasn't bad. Perhaps I don't know how to cook a goose or the bird was tough to begin with. It had to be tough after flying about two thousand miles. If anybody offers you a wild goose, do yourself a favor and refuse to take it, its not worth the trouble.

By the way, have you seen the ads in the paper offering to cook your Thanksgiving turkey including stuffing and supplying the gravy? They didn't give the price though. You know what? I think cooking the turkey at home on this day is half the fun. What is Thanksgiving without the aroma of a nice turkey cooking in your own oven? There again I might be wrong but I still think that the kids should watch you preparing your own dinner. How else are they going to learn to cook? On the other hand perhaps they shouldn't learn cooking. Just give them credit cards and let them dine out; its easy that way but no fun. By the way, if you are serving cocktails before dinner try this one; pour into a mixer with cracked ice, 1½ oz. of your favorite booze, 1 spoon sugar 2 oz. cranberry juice and mix, garnish with orange and cherry.

See you in the goose blind.

Fenner

Photo in front of the restaurant showing the Armenian connection.
From left to right– Yessi Torosian (Esther's father), Esther Fuller (Fenner's wife), Agnes Torosian (Esther's mother), Steve Stevens (Fenner's brother-in-law) and Fenner.

Gourmet Corner

By FENNER FULLER

Hello again: The editor is publishing a column entitled "Club Fronts," and to me it seems quite interesting. For instance, I mentioned some few columns ago that the Chef in a restaurant up the avenue from me would probably be serving frozen fish dishes rather than freshly caught fish—this was when they decided to start serving fish dishes along with their regular menu—and the editor had to run down there and blab out everything I had said to him. The Chef in question told the editor that he was a Lebanese and he probably knew more about Armenian cooking than I (Fenner Fuller) would ever know.. Well, he probably does. I wont dispute it with him. What he doesn't know, however, is that my Armenian cooking is the only Armenian food in the Bay Area with a Sotch accent. So there to him. This Chef also stated that I was welcome to come in to his place and enjoy one of his excellent meals at his expense so he could prove I was in error about the frozen fish. One of these nights I am going to take Mrs. Fuller and go down and see just how good this food of his is.

In the Club Fronts column, he also mentions that Chuck Coughlin has dispensed with French Cuisine. I'm glad to hear this because as far as I'm concerned French and Italian cooking is for the birds. If you doubt it, go into one of these places and order chicken or veal, and if it tastes like either of them I'll eat your hat. In the early days in Europe they had no refrigeration and most of the time the food was ready for the garbage can, so the Chefs had to cover it up with garlic, sweet basil, oregano, onions and a hundred other condiments. It became a style to cook that way and it has come down thru the ages. After all, how can you tell how food tastes when you are half crocked on red wine or sweet vermouth.

It's just like "oysters hangtown." The oysters were spoiled by the time they arrived by stage coach from the Bay Area to Placerville and the cook had to cover up the odor with bacon and eggs and onions.

Now dear reader, if you want to eat chicken that tastes like chicken, buy as many half chickens as you wish. I'd suggest two pounds cut in half. Place them on a sheet pan with oil—any kind but crank case—peanut oil is good and brush it on. No salt or pepper, place in hot oven for about one-half hour or until skin puffs up and turns golden brown. Remove from oven and place the birds in a fry pan with tight cover, add salt and pepper, half cup of white wine and cook on top of stove for fifteen minutes. You'll love it. See you at the fish fry.

—Fenner.

Photo of Darius Milhaud, French composer and teacher, watching Sotomayer along with Alexander Snyder. Milhaud dined at the restaurant.

Gourmet Corner

By FENNER FULLER

This column is primarily aimed at the rich folks who live up on the hill and who plan their regular Christmas parties again this year. Following are a list of items you might be interested in.

Most of the parties I've attended have the usual casserole dish of curried crab legs, chicken on a soggy biscuit or dried toast, so here's one that your guests will talk about for years to come;

The recipe calls for boned pheasant, but tell me, where in the world are you going to get twenty boned pheasants? Instead order twenty or thirty half chickens and treat them the same way, only why go to the trouble of taking the bones out? Bake the chicken in clay. This will also help it to retain all its flavorsome juices.

BAKED CHICKEN IN CLAY ... Wet your hands well preparatory to rolling out of the clay. Clay is rolled out about one inch thick on a sheet of waxed paper, the paper being kept damp to prevent sticking. Place wild rice risotto in cavity of chicken and fold up. The stuffed bird is then placed on a large piece of "home folks" Kaiser foil. A slice of smoked ham is laid on top of the chicken. The chicken and ham are then wrapped in the foil. Then it is placed in the center of the clay and the clay is then folded around the bird. The wax paper is peeled off the clay as it is folded around the bird.

Your clay should be shaped into a loaf and kept moist. The clay loaves may be stored in the refrigerator for two days. When ready to cook, place loaves in a pan and bake in an oven 375 to 400 degrees for about an hour. Remove, place the loaves on a board or a buffet table and let your guests crack the clay open with a hammer. You will find that none of the natural juices, flavor or aroma of the bird will be lost.

Note of warning. If the party has a tendency to get rough be careful that some goof doesn't get hold the clay and start throwing it around, it could kill you. After all they make bricks out of this stuff and that's what you'll have when it comes out of the oven. It's a good idea to have the kids stand by and pick up the pieces of clay as they are broken off the chicken. They can use this clay to make a free form, or something.

LAKE MERRITT CAVIAR ... Get a three and one half ounce jar of white fish caviar from Wisconsin, mix with a small can of chopped ripe olives, add a few spoons of olive oil and lemon juice and mix well. This is extremely good if you like caviar. The heck with the Russians, make your own at home.

See you in the clay pit.

Fenner.

Fenner constructing camel for the Nativity Scene using the design from the Camel cigarette company.

Gourmet Corner
By
Fenner Fuller

Another Christmas is here and the Park Department boys have installed the well known Natavity Scene in the Park by the Lakepark Libary. For you new readers of the Times I must tell you that this beautiful scene was built by the merchants of Grand Ave. and The Lakeshore. I can't begin to name all the men that helped build it but a few I will never forget, namely, Carl Ritzman the big shoe man on Lakeshore Ave. he was about the only man that could pound a nail straight, he above all was the best mechanic on the job, then there was the man that runs the fine delicatesen store on the ave. there was Walter Ault, his wife has a dress shop on Grand ave. he is a very fine painter and knew how to mix plaster of paris and had the know how of about everything, and God bless him, Dr. Johnson he was swell too. of course there was Lou Mouglic, John Dell and many others most of them were bosses with the exception of the first three I mentioned, Oh yes, me too, I thought up the ida and I must give thanks to the the Camel cigarett co. they supplied the design for the camels. The whole thing took about 150 man hours and about six quarts of spirets, I guess that is why the scene was such a success is because of the spirets, if you look closely at the faces on the wise men you will notice that a few of the figures are just a bit cockeyed, thats because I had too mush spirit, anyway come down and bring the kids I know they will enjoy it. Christmas dinner is so much like Thanksgiving there isn't much use of me telling you what to cook however I will give you a few easy nick-nacks for your drink snaks. Boil some chicken livers for about thirty min. drain off the liquid, put through a fine grinder with just a dash of onion and a bit of garlic, mix with your favorite mayonase, goes good on crackers and makes a fine spread. Do the same with skinless hot dogs only mix with catsup, good on crackers. Canned crab at its best isn't too hot but you can grind the meat up and treat it the same as above and it makes a good cheap Hors D' Oeuvres. After all you might have some folks over that you don't particually care much about so why waste a lot of money on them. To-day I'm going to try and write my Christmas when I was a kid,

12-18-63

back in New England. Really folks, there isn't much to write about because
XMAS didn't mean too much to us on the farm, If you ever experanced a winter in
New England around Christmas time it generally snowed or we would have a
blizzard or it would be twenty below outside and in weather like this
a person doesn't feel like celebrating, for instance the first one up in
the morning had to shovel a path to the privy and there was always a snow
drift about four to six feet deep between the wood shed and the corn crib,
this task was no joke and to would knock the Christmas spirit out of anyone.
However about a week or two before Christmas Mother would take me to Pawtucket and Providence to see Santa Claus, it was fun looking at all the
wonderful toys, Mama would con the salesman to let me get up on the rocking
horse and take a couple rocks back and fourth, boy I could have stayed for
ever on it, I was really too small to look to see what was on the counters,
once in a while Mama would lift me up ## see all the wonders of toyland,
every once in a while I would ask for something and I would always get the
same stock answer, IF you are a GOOD boy PERHAPS Santa will bring them to
you. Really folks, I don't remember ever being bad, but I guess I was because I never got what I asked for, I remember the stores were crowded and it
was my custom to follow mother all around the stores, it sure was a drag, I
used to hold onto her skirt and it was no fun, I couldn't see anything except fat fannys, just my eye level, after trapseing through the sea of fannys
I didn't care about Santa, toys or anything, once I got hold of the wrong skirt
and got lost, I thought it might be the wrong one because this lady walked
to fast, anyway I started to lag back, couldn't keep the pace up, she felt
me tugging at her skirt, she looked down at me and shook me off as though I
wild cat or something, after shaking me off she left me standing there I was
nudged by knees and rumps to a clearing in the notion dept. and some tall
bald headed man with a folwer (LOWER) in his buttonhole picked me up and asked me what
my name was, I said, Fenner, Fenner who he asked, I didn't know, he stood me
up on the McCalls pattern counter and in about a half hour mother spotted me
standing there with a candy cane that the nice lady at the counter gave me.
Mother was sure suprised to seem me there, You know, Mother was such a

USE FOR 12-25-63

shopper I doubt if she even missed me, anyway, I was happy to see her.
I have a vivid memory or Gordon, Elmer and Delmont and myself going up to
to the big pasture and cutting down a Christmas tree, I don't know the name
of the tree, it looked like the ones we have out here in the grave yards, I
think it was cedar or something, anyway we would decorate it with strings of
pop corn and cranberries, also colored paper rings that we stuck together
with paste made of flour and water, we also had multi colored candles, that we
did't dare to light because these trees used to burn like kerosene. Anyway it
looked good to us. As I remember I was the youngest kid and was the
only one that believed in Santa Claus, and at that tender age I even had
my doubts, so the night before Christmas I hung my stocking up by the fire
place and went to bed with dreams of all the things I wanted, rocking horse
and all. I was up bright and early in the A.M. and went directly to the stocking, only to find some nuts that I had gathered in the fall, a few pieces
of coal and a few sticks of wood, and three oranges, coal, wood and nuts
didn't thrill me too much and as for oranges, I didn't care for them either because
Mother used to mix orange juice with castor oil and to this day I dislike
oranges except in Screw drivers. I later asked Papa why the coal and wood
and his answer was, coal and wood is much more valuable than toys, you know
he was right, remember it WAS cold out side. I would then scamper over to the
tree and to my surprise, a cast iron fire truck, it wasn't a truck it was a
beautiful Hook and ladder with four galloping iron horses, boy was that something
it had a fireman driving the horses and a man on the tiller in the rear, another
marvel of the age was a metal top that used to give off beautiful music when
you would spin it, there was also a metal drum with a clown on top that would
do a gig when you wound it, also I got a steet car that you would wind up and
it would go round and round untill by brothers wound it too tight and busted
it. So it was a beautiful Christmas after all.

So untill next Christmas, I'll see you in the manger.

Fenner.

Cover of weekly county magazine showing the Nativity Scene.

Gourmet Corner
By
Fenner Fuller

How nice Grand Ave. and Lakeshore Avenues look this Christmas, the decoration committies should be thanked. However, I got a swell idea for next year, its not my idea though, I got it from the town of St. Helena Calif. and I think its great. They have taken all the parking meters off the stands for the Christmas shoppers and replaced the meters with Xmas trees. Can you realize what a boon this would be for the merchants? I can and I, for one, think we should start the ball rolling for next year. KOSHER?. Yep, this is me writing, figure this one out, a Yankee telling you how to make (KREPLACH). This is a filling. 3 cups cooked chicken meat, I med. onion sauteed golden, 2 hard boiled eggs, salt and pepper to taste. Grind all the above ingredients very fine. Now my dear hearts, heres another dilly. Caviar blintzes. This is for twenty four blintzes. 8 in. blintzes (cut 6 wedges to each). On each wedge of blintz dough, put I teaspoon black caviar. Then sprinkle with chopped chives and parsley and add a touch of lemon juice. Fold and roll to shape. Heat in slow oven until warm.

You should live so long. A customer of ours comes in about twice a month, perhaps tats all he can stand, anyway two weeks ago he celebrated his IOI yrs. birthday. He carries a cane, and doesn't use it, he told me he just uses it to chase the dogs away. Mrs. Fuller asked him last week how he was feeling. Now get this. He told her he wasn't feeling too good. Esther asked him what was the matter and his answer was this, I have a tooth ache. Now what do you kids think of that? Shows you what happens to folks that eat here with me. By the way, he always eats lamb, so there you beef and potatoe eaters.

By the way, I haven't cooked any KOSHER food here, I just do this at home when we have company, so please forgive me if I dont serve the blintzes in my restaurant. The reason, too much work. Armenian and Arab is enough for one joint. Well Happy Hollidays ahead for all.

See you in the funny paper.

Fenner.

Photos of Fenner at the Mardikian ranch enjoying the cows.

Gourmet Corner
By
Fenner Fuller

Hey there, Did I ever tell you about the time I wanted to raise "Buffalo" up on Geo. Mardikians ranch in St. Helena? You know what? George was all for sending me back to the Dakotas and buying up a herd, however when I fould out what it was going to cost for fencing I forgot about it up till now. I still think its a swell deal. George being a much better business man than I asked, how we going to make any money on Buffalo, well George I said, just give me some more Iced tea on the rocks and I will tell you, very glad you asked. As you know my friend, there are many lodges in this country, The Elks, The Moose, and several others but to my knoledge there are no (BUFFALO LODGES) so my friend we can organize about fifty thousand units in the U.S. and sell each lodge room a Buffalo Head, at about three hundred per copy, then for parades and special functions each member should have a Buffalo Robe, get it George? Go on he said, then theres the meat, we could sell it to the freezer happy boys, also in the summer we could gather up all the buffalo chips and sell them for barbequing the steaks, This would be called a (PARIE COOK OUT) wouldn't that be something, just think what it would be like if about fifty families were having a real Parie cook out using the real fuel of the parie, how would you like to live down wind from these happy Buffalo eaters using Buffalo chips for fuel especially if you lived in a low pressure area. This organization would be cslled United States Order Of Buffalos, for short (U.S.O.O.B), we could even sell the members Buffalo teeth for their watch fobs, or perhaps the women folks would go for a charm bracelet made of the small teeth. Iv'e thought of many things to get the U.S.O.O.B. started such as low cost insurance, for instance, if each member bought fifty sacks of chips per year we could give him $1,000 insuranse, each sack would sell for one buck, we could give them low low cost bural, no casket, just a Buffalo hide, the paid up members would only pay fifty bucks , the bural to the dedicated Buffalo boys would be in North Decato Parie. Any of you dear hearts want to invest in some heavy fencing, or perhaps you know how to stuff a Buffalo, I don't.Oh, one more though to make a million, Canned Buffalo meat for your pets, much better than horse meat. Here it is girls, Barbecue Sause for Buffalo, One cup katsup, 2 tablespoons vinegar, 2 T.S. Worcestershire sauce, ¼ tea spoon Tabasco sauce, ½ cup chopped onion, I t.s. Dry mustard, ½ t.s. salt. I cup water. Mix ingredients in sauce pan, allow to boil and then reduce heat and simmer for ten minuts. if too thick add a bit more water.
Well folks, see you at the lodge.   fenner.

Fenner giving a cooking class in the restaurant kitchen for students from Mills College.

Gourmet Corner
By
Fenner Fuller

RE-WRITE

Whatter you know, City Hall reads my column, this morning I had a visit From Mr. Fred C. Stapleton of the public works dept. in other words he is foreman for the street and engineering dept. and a very nice fellow at that, a real Oakland booster and dedicated to keeping our beautiful city clean. He came to me in regards to the column I wrote about the street sweeper putting the leaves in the storm drain, you know what, he thanked me for my civic pride and intrest in the city, we came to the conclusion that it really wasn't the sweepers fault for getting rid of the leaves the best way he could, the reason he did this is because there were not litter cans in the block, and to get rid of the leaves he would have to eat them or carry them about a block, so now we are going to have a brand new litter can in the block., you see We at the Times do some good for the city. Speaking of litter cans, I had no ida that they were such a problem and costly to thr tax payer, This guy Stapelton has some very good ideas that I hope in the future this new type can will be standard in the city, so with the help FROM the Merchants associations and the Street Maintenance Division we might come up with something big. The thought just came to me, wouldn't it be nice if Oakland had some beautiful young girls roaming the streets and tapping everybody on the shoulder if they littered the sidewalks, we could call them (THE CAN CAN GIRLS) not a bad ida for the junior leagues daughters., enough of civic pride jazz. LENT will soon be here so here is a dish you might like, Go over to the Lake View Market on Grand and buy a package of Cape Cod scollops, thaw out, flatten them out with the side of a cleaver, don't hit them too hard or they will go to pieces, just enough to make them lay flat, place in pie tin, add salt pepper, cracker crumbs, butter and some sherry wine and water, place under a broiler and cook untill brown should take you about tem min. serve with rice or potatoes, tossed salad and a jug of chablis, any good brand. I hate to say this but the new fountain in the park is for the birds, no not even for the birds, because thay cant take a bath in it., The designer got a good start but forgot to put something in the center, such as a High sphere or a pole with large dicks with water trickeling down makeing it somethin we can see when we ride by. What do you say fellows, shall we all get together some week end and build something, We can sneak it in some week end when the park boys are on vacation, after its up they woldn't take it down, cost too much. Remember the Camels, we did that and the Park Dept. is stuck with it. Ho Ho well its a thought.

See you next week in the (can) Litter can I mean.

Fenner.

Correspondence from friends who were serving as ambassadors from Brazil to Japan and enjoyed eating at the restaurant.

Gourmet Corner
By
Fenner Fuller

Gosh Old Hemlock; I had to turn away six people last Saturday evening, the reason being, I was too crowded and there was too long a wait. What griped me was that these folks, to me were V.I.Ps. He is feature writer for the San Francisco Chronical, his name is John Campbell Bruce or is it J. Bruce Campbell, anyway take your pick, something like my name, Fenner Adouphus Cahmberlain Fuller, like John, take your pick, I will answer to any of them. I really wanted to talk to this guy, because I thought he could give me some pointers on how to write this column, on the other hand, what good would it do, I can't spell and I have a hard job putting the commers, in the right places, Gosh I wish I wasn't such a lover when I was going to school, anyway I LEARNED a lot about girls, I wonder if John Bruce Campbell does, at my age I wish I could write and the heck with the girls, I have a hunch that John knows about both, judgeing from his beautiful wife. About seventeen years ago a young couple came in for dinner, they would come about three time a week, we struck up an aquaintance and a very lovely one at that. He was vice Consel from Brazil, he was transfered to Washington, and was on his way up inthe Diplomatic service of his Country, anyway, last Friday he and his wife and beautiful three children came in and had dinner, sort of a surprise, he brought twelve guests with him, He and his family were on their way to Japan, he is now Ambassitor from Brazil to Japan, not a bad job ### ### for a young guy, I only hope the his Brazulian money will be good in Japan, if not I guess he can use credit cards, good luck John Pinero, I hope to see you in the baths in Tokio, Let the fat girl bathe me, you take the skinney one. Oh. by the way, I hear they are going to do something about the "Fountain Of Youth", when I don't know, As you know they should do something soon, I know they will, they all WORK hard at the Park Dept. to do the right thing, the only trouble is they don't consult the Art Commission about the beauty of Oakland. I don't know what it cost to run a neon sign but I think the Grand Lake Theatre should turn on their beautiful siagn even if the merchants #on Grand Ave. and Lakeshore Ave have to pay part of the light bill, Its a good add for this district. (Kansas Swiss Steak, Mix together I tablespoon dry mustard with ½ half cup flour, pound the mixture into I½ lb. I in. thick, this should be top round steak. Season with salt and pepper and brown on both sides in hot fat. Place meat in small roaster, and pour over the following; I cup sliced onions, I tabelspoon of brown sugar, I tabelspoon Worcestershire sauce, I carrot diced, I ½ cups canned tomatoes, cover and bake slow in oven 325Deg. for about I½ hrs. serves six.
So long, see you in the fountain of youth, Fenner.

Photos of Lake Merritt, Oakland, CA. Top photo shows Esther and Eldora (Fenner's cousin). The second and third photos are from Fenner's apartment.

Gourmet Corner
By
Fenner Fuller

As our great American, Will Rodgers used to say, "ALLS I KNOW IS WHAT I READ IN THR PAPERS" While looking for the funny paper in our oversized Shoppers special paper I came accross an item where one of our tallest City councelmen wanted to dig up part of the park and have underground parking, Didn't anybody tell the councel about my plan of draining Lake Merritt and putting under water parking in the Lake and having moveable sidewalks run to differant parts of the City, As I said years ago this could be done and we could have parking and the lake to, if they are intrested I will give them my plan, no charge, just give Lakeshore and Grand Ave. merchants the consession on the gas and oil. Funny why the City Councel don't ask me about these things, because they must know by now that(I'M THE GREATEST) Wow. Then I read where they dedicated the new County Building, they Had to say the prayers, a Rabi and a Priest, where in the world were the Seventh Day Adventist and the Babtist, also the Mormans, Oh well , we A.PAs will have our day in Heaven I "Guess". Oh, by the way I read that our great "Emperor" of the East Bay got married, good luck, some day I predict that he will be "KING" of Oakland, so keep diging boy. Speaking of boys, did you read where Cacusses Clay or what ever his name is, droped his name and wants to be called "ALI OPPS" or something, can you feature him going into the ring and having some rag head sing chants from way up in the balcony And our boy putting down a prayer rug, faceing the East and praying to Allah boy, that would be better that Georgous George with the "FLIT GUN"., Boy hes The Greatest, The Army thinks he is the "GREATEST DOPE". I had better quit this kind of talk or I'll be put in jail, boy would that be a releafe. Easter Sunday is here and I would like to put an add in this paper but every time I put and add in somebody burys it in the paper someplace, I can't even find it myself, anyway if I don't put an add in, just for you dear hearts I will be open from one till nine P.M. serving a delicious dinner so there Mr. Masterson , However if you don't go out to eat, this is what I would have at home for Sunday, perhaps you would like it too. Before going to the Sun Rise Services or early morning Mass I would just have orange juice coffee and one small piece of toast, after services I would go home and grill a full sized slice of Smithfield ham, thats the kind they cure in Kentucky or Virginia, along with two eggs fried in butter, toast, orange marmalaid and coffee. Then I would lay down, read the papers and take a nap for about two hours., At about four o'clock I would put a leg of spring lamb in the oven, fix some mashed potatoes and ##### peas cooked in olive oil and onion, small slice of appel pie. Well If I were the women of the house I would say, lets not bother with all this and lets go down to Fenners and have dinner and leave the dishes to him. Ho hum.
By the way, did you notice that there were more Green Flags out on the I7th than they were Red White and Blue on the 4th of July?
Well enough for now, see all you tax dodgers in jail.

Fenner.

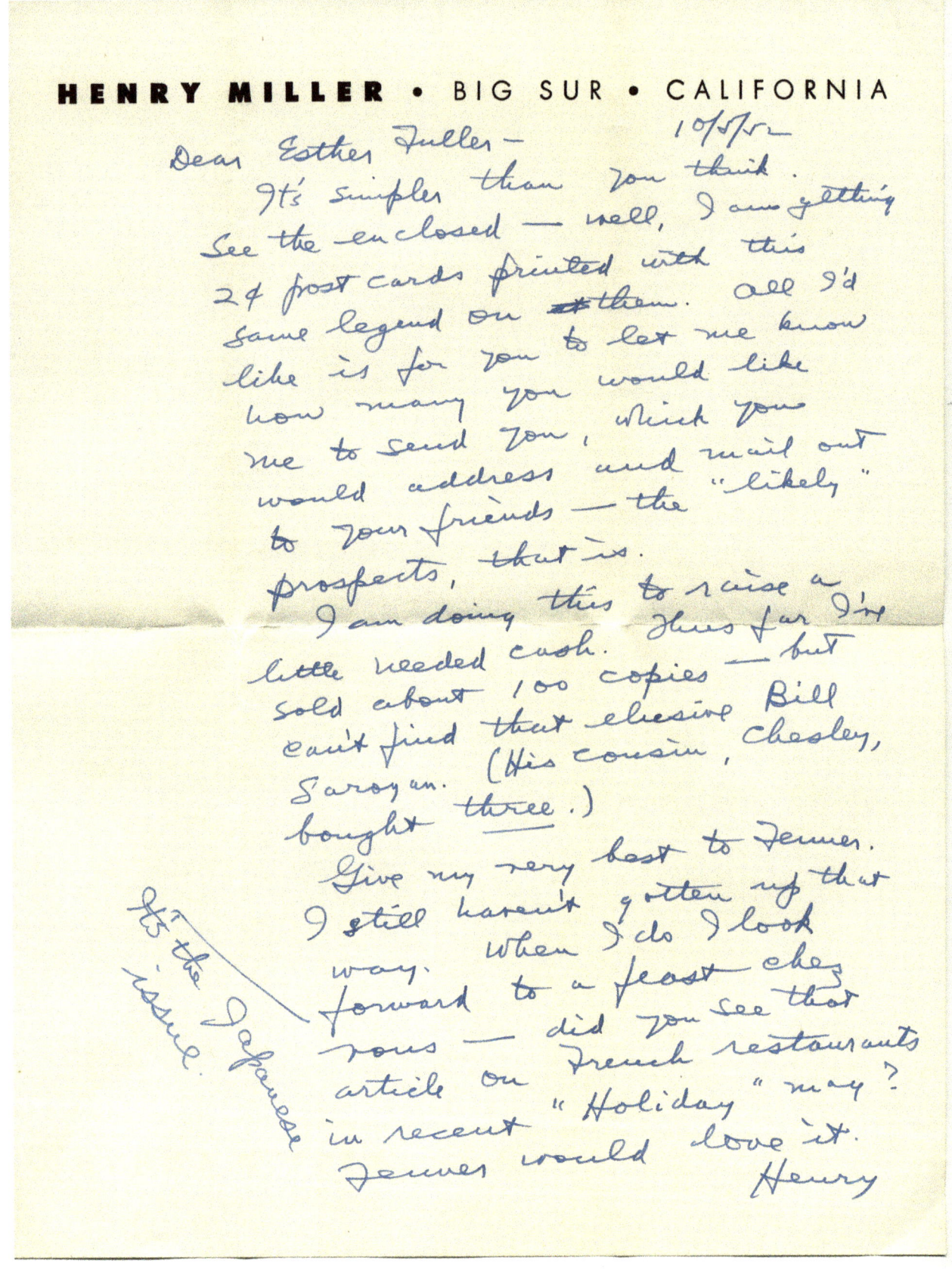

HENRY MILLER • BIG SUR • CALIFORNIA

Dear Esther Fuller — 10/5/52

It's simpler than you think. See the enclosed — well, I am getting 24 post cards printed with this same legend on them. All I'd like is for you to let me know how many you would like me to send you, which you would address and mail out to your friends — the "likely" prospects, that is.

I am doing this to raise a little needed cash. Thus far I've sold about 100 copies — but can't find that elusive Bill Saroyan. (His cousin, Chesley, bought three.)

Give my very best to Fenner. I still haven't gotten up that way. When I do I look forward to a feast chez vous — did you see that article on French restaurants in recent "Holiday" — may? Fenner would love it.

Henry

It's the Japanese issue.

Correspondence from author/friend Henry Miller who ate at the restaurant.

Gourmet Corner

By FENNER FULLER

Before I forget it, (which I don't think I will) if you happen to be in downtown Oakland, stop in and sample the wares at the **Egg Shop** and **Apple Press**. You will find it at 382 17th St. It's a most delightful little restaurant and they have delicious omelettes. The apple juice is also very good. The fellow that owns it is an Armenian and he not only cooks, he is an artist, a playwrite and evidently a carpenter along with it because he built the place himself and made all the fixtures for it. Better not go there during the lunch hour as it is practically impossible to get in at that time due to the crowds, try a little later in the afternoon. You can eat there for about the price of a large bag of potato chips.

•

Well, what do you know? I received two checks back from Municipal Court today. Overpaid my traffic tickets. Now wasn't that nice of the coppers after all the mean things I've said about them in the past. It's enough to make a body hang their head in shame.

An excellent suggestion for the Park Department would be to plant the kind of ivy that grows on walls and cover the MacArthur overpass with it. That's the one on Grand and Lakeshore avenues. Besides it would be just great for Oakland to have the largest and most beautiful ivy covered pigeon roost in the world.

•

I paid five bucks for a book on how to prepare hors de oeuvres and on page 18 I came across this little gem that I wouldn't dare try myself but I'm going to pass it on to you. Get this.

PEANUT BUTTER CHILI SAUCE DIP: 1¼ cups of smooth or chunk peanut butter, 1¼ cups chili sauce. Blend together until smooth and refrigerate until ready. Well there it is. You try it, I'm not going to.

Here's another lulu. **OYSTER KABOB:** Use small oysters, sprinkle them with lemon juice, salt and pepper and thread on small skewers with bacon strips and button mushrooms. I'll bet you ten to one that the oysters fall off the skewer before they're cooked. Guess I'll send the book back and use my own common sense. I'll get farther that way.

•

I believe I mentioned in a former column that a lady once told me she didn't read my column because it was so much mish-mash. I don't know what mish-mash is but if it's anything like this column today, then I know what it is. This is a real mish-mash. Incidentally how could she know it was mish-mash unless she had read it to begin with? Well, so long. See you under the ivy covered pigeon roost.

Fenner Adolphus Fuller.

Fenner at the Mardikian ranch.

Fenner's last column - April 29-1964

Gourmet Corner

By FENNER FULLER

What does a gourmet eat? Well, I'll tell you. George Mardikian (he of Omar Khayyam's fame) and I, went up to his ranch at St. Helena last Sunday evening and arrived home early Wednesday a.m.

While we were at the ranch we decided to cook up a bash of food and George asked me what I would like to indulge in.

"Well, I replied, "What I'd like is some plain boiled beef with horse radish sauce."

"My boy," he said, "That's what you shall have." So we went into St. Helena proper and loaded up at the grocery store.

He bought some beef shank cut up in large pieces and after we got back to the ranch he put the beef in a pot covered it with water and put it to boil for about three hours, adding some onion, salt and pepper and that's all. Well I'm here to tell all hands that it tasted like ambrosia to me. He also served some 'horse beans' that he had planted and they tasted very good. We did go overboard on our diet and had a couple of slices of french bread with our meal and one can of beer each.

The next morning I got up at 5:30 a.m., the reason for this being the birds woke me up. They're kind of nice to get woke up by. I went down to the lake and caught a couple of nice bass which I cleaned and put in the refrigerator after I got back to the ranch. I then saddled up a horse and took a nice two hour ride around the ranch. I got back in time to hear the cook (Geo.) ringing the breakfast bell.

Guess what he had cooked up. Yep, you guessed it. He fried the bass and made a delicious sauce with water cress, lemon and parsley, and a dash of chablis wine thickened with arrowroot. I tell you, nothing's too good for the working class.

Besides getting a fish hook imbedded in my thumb that I couldn't get out myself, George gave me an overdose of brandy, sterilized a razor blade, and cut the darn thing out. So far it's a good job, no blood poisoning yet. I'll let you know when my thumb drops off.

Well that's the way we gourmets eat so don't be afraid to buy the low cost boiling beef.

Here's a favorite breakfast dish of George's that you might like. SCRAMBLED EGGS WITH TOMATOES ... Here is a perfect dish for those in search of an effective natural laxative. It's also a favorite Near East breakfast dish.

Use one tomato and two eggs per person. Peel and chop tomato, saute in butter, add salt and pepper. Break eggs directly into the tomatoes and stir constantly while cooking. The eggs will set in about one minute. This dish was taken from the book, "Dinner at Omar Khayyam's", by Geo. Mardikiand.

Well, I guess I've said enough about my friend for one day so will close with these few words: "Make reservations early for Mother's day. Bring Mother to dinner."

I could think of a dandy closing line for this column but I know what our pious editor would do with it, so I'll skip it and see you in the boiling beef department in the market.

Recipes that might work

By FENNER FULLER

SHISH KABAB

Leg of Lamb
2 large Onions
2 tb. Cumin Seed
1 tb. Ground Rosemary
1 tb. Salt
1 tsp. Black Pepper
1/2 cup Cooking Oil
1 cup Sherry Wine

Cut excess fat from lamb. Remove bone and cut lamb into squares from 1½ to 2 inches. Chop onion fine and mix with lamb. Add to this, cumin seed, rosemary, salt, pepper, oil and sherry wine. Let stand over night. When ready to cook, place on skewers and broil for ten minutes in either electric, gas or charcoal broiler.
That's it!
P.S. If it doesn't turn out right, throw it away and bring the family to Fenner Fuller for dinner. OR --- you can always eat ham and eggs.

PACIFIC BROILED OYSTERS

Place 1 pint of small to medium sized oysters in a pie tin. Season to taste - salt, pepper and paprika. Sprinkle 2 tb. breadcrumbs over entire mixture. Add 1 tb. butter, 3 oz. white wine. Place under broiler for 5 minutes. Baste occasionally. Serve with your favorite starch.

My idea of cooking beef, ham or poultry is to cook it in the "raw" and Not add any seasonings until after meat or poultry has been cooked. Many condiments, particularly salt, tend to dry out or dehydrate meat, therefore, the following tips:

Cook a ham just as it comes from the market. Here's an excellent sauce

Mock Champagne Sauce

Heat 1 can apple juice thickened slightly with corn starch. Add 1 tb. brown sugar, 1/2 bottle gingerale. That's all!! Wonderful sauce over ham.

INCLUDING MILK $1.35

WE CATER TO BANQUETS AND PARTIES

*Good luck
have fun
Fenner C. Fuller*

LAMB SHANKS.

Wash lamb shanks-put in large pan-
salt, pepper, sweet paprika to taste-
tomato sauce.   Water to cover lamb
shanks.
Bake in oven 2 hours or more after
it comes to a boil (about 3 hours)
Lamb shanks should start to brown
on top.

[handwritten: flat / probably 3/4 # tomato sauce]

POT ROAST.

Bottom Round -
   Trim inside tough strip and all
skin and sides - cut into 3 pieces
lengthwise.
Brown in large pan with Wesson oil
(about pint).
Take out meat -
make gravy with about two heaping
cups of flour - brown - pan meat
has been braised - pour water,-
salt, pepper - place 3 pieces meat.
keep meat covered with gravy while
it cooks - 2 or 3 hours.   Cover.

TART LEMON PIE

3 eggs
1½ c. Sugar
1 Lemon Rind and whole juice
1/4 c. extra lemon juice

Mix and bake
1½ c. Flour
1½ tsp. Sugar
1 tsp. Salt
½ c. Oil
2 tb. milk

Mix milk and oil first
add rest of ingredients
then pat into pie shell

RUM MOCHA PIE
Graham Cracker-Butter-Sugar Crust

20 Marshmallows) melted
¼-cup Milk   )

Add pinch Salt and 2 tb. Cocoa

3 tb. Rum

Fold in 1 cup Whipped Cream

Lemon Torte

4 egg whites — beat with wire whip until frothy
¼ tsp. cream of tarter — beat until it peaks
1 cup sugar — beat until thick and glossy.

Pour in greased 9" pie tin and bake one hour and ten minutes: 20 minutes at 275° and rest at 300°

Filling

4 egg yolks beaten
½ cup sugar
2 lemon rinds
4 tbs lemon juice (add 3 + taste)
pinch salt

Cook until thick, then cool

1 cup cream — whipped

Add ½ cream to custard & spread over merangue, spread remainder of cream on top and let stand 24 hours

Snow Pudding

2 T Knox gelatin dissolved in
½ C warm water & set in hot water to dissolve
1 t vanilla or lemon
¾ C sugar
3 egg whites beaten stiff. Add sugar gradually, then gelatin & beat all for 15 minutes and set aside to stiffen

Custard

1 pt. milk
(can add a little grated orange rind)
3 egg yolks
½ C sugar
Dash salt
vanilla

Stir together & put over hot water until it coats the spoon

IRENE'S UPSIDE-DOWN CHOCOLATE PUDDING.

- 1 cup Flour
- 2 tsp. Baking Powder.
- 1/2 tsp. Salt
- 3/4 Cup Sugar
- 3 tbs. Cocoa.
- 1 tsp Vanilla.
- 1/2 Cup milk, or eveporated milk (1/2 water)
- 2 Tbs. Salad oil or melted shortening.
- 1/2 Cup coarsly chopped nuts, any kind.
- 1 and 1/4 cups brown sugar.
- 1/4 Cup Cocoa.
- 2 cups hot water.

****

Sift flour, measure; add Baking powder, salt, sugar, and the 3 tbsp. of Cocoa, and sift together into a mixing bowl. Add vanilla to milk, then add this-- with salad oil or shortening and chopped nuts-- to the dry ingredients. Stir until well blended. Turn into a square pan (8x8x2) Mix the brown sugar and the 1/4 cup cocoa. Sprinkle this mixture over the batter. Pour the hot water over the entire surface. Bake in moderate oven--350--for 40 to 45 minutes. Spoon out while warm, with the Chocolate sauce. SUPER with whipped cream.

Baked Cranberry

1 Bag Ocean Spray Cranberry (3 cups)
3 c sugar
1½ - 2 tsp ground cinnamon
1 tsp   "   Clove
3 or 4 T.B. grated orange peel
¼ - ⅓ c orange juice
Juice of 1 lemon -
Bake 1 hr. in oven (medium)

Orange Sauce -

Make a very heavy syrup add unpealed thinly sliced oranges. Cook until the white of the orange is transparent (in color) - If the syrup seems too thin remove oranges and cook the syrup to desired consistency -

Art

MIRIAM DUNGAN CROSS
Tribune Art Critic

ARTIST AND FRIEND

The sudden death of Fenner Fuller shocked and saddened the many friends who have known him over the years as the most resilient, generous and honest of men. Witty columnist, keen observer, robust raconteur and great cook, Fenner embraced the arts as well to please his artist wife Esther and in so doing proved his own talent.

Member of the Mills College Ceramic Guild, he won wide recognition for his ceramic clowns often created in demonstrations at art festivals and fairs. He refused to sell a single one. They were perhaps his children, a Pagliacci part of himself. These fluid, activated little figures have a poignancy beyond the painted surfaces of their faces. Children (our own now grown daughter included) adored him whether he was "rattling the rocks" in their heads, showing them how he made clowns or letting them handle the clay.

Fenner further demonstrated his talent in painting direct, exuberant circus scenes. He also designed and made the wonderfully expressive life-size figures as well as objects in the huge Nativity scene shown every Christmas in Lakeside Park opposite his restaurant. He rejoiced in the fact that the restaurant is also the Fenner Fuller Gallery and the site of frequent gatherings of figures in art from over the country, although he claimed much of the avant-garde work Esther selected was beyond him. However, shortly before his death as he was expertly concocting Bloody Marys, he carried on a running commentary on bull fighting, ranching, writing (his own and Lucius Beebe's) and art including a perceptive critique on a Robert Downs abstraction hanging nearby.

God bless him and his bright spirit.—M.D.C.

"off the record"
BILL MASTERSON

The Clown Maker is gone.

Seems like rather an inept manner in which to describe the death of a man, but in the case of Fenner Adolphus Chamberlain Fuller it is the most fitting simile I could think of to describe him.

His passing was in direct contrast to his way of living.

He retired to sleep last Wednesday evening and sometime during the wee hours his poor, overworked heart gave out and he gave up the unequal struggle for existence and relinquished his soul to his maker.

Thus passed from our midst a vital influence in the lives of most of us.

Fenner Fuller was an influence in the lives of many of the merchants of both Lakeshore and Grand avenues, as well as the lives of literally thousands of friends. His flambouyant personality made itself felt wherever he went. His feeling for human life, for beauty, for creativity was deeply expressed in his weekly column in the pages of this paper. Fenner called them as he saw them. If he trod on any toes it was entirely unintentional, the man just didn't have it in him to deliberately hurt a soul. I could spend hour upon hour expounding upon the virtues of this great man (I was closer to him than many publishers are with their writers) but I think it best to exemplify the kind of man Fenner was by presenting brief opinions from those who knew him well over a period of many years as a merchant and developer of the Grand Lake scene . . .

FENNER

From Yates Bleuel of Bleuel Hardware, **"A Character;"** George Cawog of George's Shirts, **"Happy;"** Howard Reed of Reed's For Beauty, **"Witty;"** Ethel LaGasa, Edy's Candies, **"Great;"** Elaine Baker, Edy's **"Down to Earth;"** Walter Bennett, Bennett's Cameras, **"Unpredictably Chaming;"** Geo. Gundlach, The Place, **"Genial;"** Leonard Moss, Dolphin Liquors, **'Exceptionall Likeable;"** Ida Hockins, Hockins

Yarn Shop, "**Jovial-Charming;**" Shadow Jory, Imperial Restaurant, "**Openhearted;**" Verdine Tomlin, Secretarial Service, "**Terrific;**" Carl Ritzman, Ritzman's Shoes, '**Humanitarian;**" Will Robertson, Wheatley's Stationary, "**Gourmet;**" Frank Curotto, Lakeshore Delicatessen, "**Funny As A Crutch;**" Sam Kaufman, Dime and Dollar Store, "**Excellent Sense Of Humor;**" Dave and Medora Stead, Lakeshore Health Foods, "**Lovable;**" Al Lobello, City Planning Commissioner, '**Active-Civic-An Expert Public Relations Man Not Working At The Business;**" -Jim Souza, Oscars Bar and Lounge, "**Effervescent;**" Ellen Stafford, Pricilla's Bakery, "**Versatile;**" Joe Bettencourt, Lorene O'Dale's Salon of Beauty, "**Fabulous;**" Bill Betancourt, Mngr. Berkeley Savings and Loan, "**Friendly;**" Del Davis, Black and White Liquors, "**Excellent Cook;**" Ken and Elmer Young, Young's Photography, "**Enjoyable;**" George Javedis, Food Town Meats, "**A Real Gentleman;**" From Pete Christoffersen, also of Foodtown Meat Market, "**Hospitable;**" Bob Kaprilian, Lakeshore Mailman, "**Energetic;**" Art Johnson, owner Stier Drugs, "**A Great Guy;**" Ray Rule, Rule's Pharmacy, "**Superb.**"

And so they go, from Lakeshore to Grand avenue, where the feeling is much the same as witnessed by such references as, "**A Zest For Living,**" from Lou Moglich, Manager of the Bank of America; from Marcel Baruch of Marcel's Music, "**Jocund, Jocose;**" Lenny Fisher, Modern Art Studios, "**Fun Loving;**" Maxine Roberts, Maxine's Jewelry "**Pagliacci;**" Gary Burgess, Grand avenue barber, "**Esoteric Soul;**" Rudy Washburn, Intercity Mortgage, "**Colorful-Urbane;**" Leah Strause, Jeff's Donuts, "**An Enigma;**" Jeff Strause, "**Tops;**" Phil Kramm, Decorator Paints, "**A Great Guy;**" Walter Jensen, Mngr. Central Valley National Bank, "**Generous;**" Al Bennett, Colonial Donuts, "**Lovable;**" Dick Seymour, Colonial Donuts, "**Fun Loving;**" Daisy Shackleford, Little Daisy of Lakeshore, "**Gregarious**" . . .

Perhaps Maxine Roberts best described Fenner with her smashing "**Pagliacci.**" For Fenner was a Pagliacci, outwardly gay, smiling, happy, carefree, apparently without a trouble in the world. Yet this man suffered much and the tears he shed he hid from public view. He was extremely sensitive, quick to feel hurt, often hurt others, was sometimes blasphemous, quick with retorts and a master of repartee. Yet Fenner was the first to apologize if he knew he had hurt you and I have seen tears in his eyes when he apologized and I was amazed at the depth of emotion in this man.

Farewell to you, Oh wonderful Pagliacci, wherever you are. I will miss you deeply and the many friends you left behind will be a little less happy for the loss of you.

Mrs. Esther Fuller
614 Grand Avenue
Oakland   94610

The PIEDMONTER

THE ONLY NEWSPAPER DEVOTED EXCLUSIVELY TO THE NEWS OF PIEDMONT

Vol. 52, No. 50   December 13, 1967 (Two Sections)   Single Copies 10c

Fenner Fuller's—A Grand Avenue Landmark—To Close Sunday

Fenner Fuller's — a landmark restaurant at 614 Grand Avenue since 1945 — will close following the dinner hour this Sunday.

Mrs. Esther Fuller, in making the announcement, said that the over 1,000 ceramic clowns made by the late Mr. Fuller, would be sent to permanent collections in various museums.

The restaurant served as a crossroads meeting place for many great people traveling through here, Mrs. Fuller commented. The Paganini Quartet had its first meals there when they arrived from Belgium; Baron Rothschild came there for his favorite Armenian food; Joe E. Brown named it among his Bay Area dining spots, also many contemporary notables, the late Henry Kaiser, Henry Miller and Darius Milhaud.

The menu, perfected by Mr. Fuller before he opened the restaurant on Feb. 3, 22 years ago, has remained unchanged since that time.

Mrs. Fuller, whose artistry is in the field of sculpting whereas Mr. Fuller's was in the perfection of gourmet cooking, kept up enthusiasm of many fledgling artists by showing their work for the first time. She is listed in Who's Who of American Women and Who's Who in America for her art work.

Mr. Fuller originated and designed the Nativity figures now being shown in the display in Lakeside Park.

Mrs. Fuller is a former member of the Library and Museum Commission, was a guiding force in the selection of the architects for the new museum, on the board of directors of the Oakland Museum Association, a member of the S. F. Art Association and the Mills Ceramic Guild.

"I am leaving business at a time when Oakland's future looks bright and shining," Mrs. Fuller told The Piedmonter. "I couldn't be more enthusiastic about it. All these past years I've been a part of Oakland's preparation for this emergence — the high-rise apartments, the new museum, BART, the new junior college, the Coliseum — the good architecture being used in some of the buildings. And I keep thinking what an exciting time for Oakland."

Mrs. Fuller lives on Merritt Avenue overlooking the lake. She says she has travel in mind, probably about Easter time, but that it will take her that long to properly take care of 22 years' collection of memorabilia so handsomely displayed through the years at the popular dining spot.

A Link to Days of Old to Close Doors

By BOB UMPHRESS

Fenner Fuller's Restaurant, at 614 Grand Ave., will serve its last meal tomorrow.

For 22½ years it has been as much a hobby as a business to those who ran it and a personal experience to those who dined there.

The restaurant opened Feb. 3, 1945, and with no advertising other than a notice painted on the window, it experienced instant success — Naval personnel, bored with the paucity of restaurants in Oakland at that time, flocked to the place and responded to its dining room informality.

With the end of the war, the servicemen vanished and their place was taken by the old Eastbay families — particularly on Thursday nights, the maid's night out.

("There was a different style of living then," reminisces Mrs. Fenner Fuller.)

These people remained loyal customers over the years. They rejected the plush new dining establishments going up in Oakland in favor of the high ceilings, straight-backed chairs and the gentility of Fenner Fuller's.

They are survivors of an age that is passing, when dining out was an event in its own right; a personal greeting at the door, an acquaintance with the waitress and refined dinner-table conversation were a very important part of life.

MRS. FENNER FULLER PACKS AWAY CLOWNS
Her restaurant-cum-art gallery closes tomorrow

These people knew instinctively what the late Fenner Fuller meant when he wrote a little reminder on the menu that taking children to a restaurants was a necessary part of their education.

Fenner Fuller himself was a big, gregarious man with a folksiness and ever-present good humor. He was in the words of his widow, Esther, a frustrated actor.

"That's why he loved restaurants," she says. "He had an audience every night."

He was the type of man who could meet the Baron Edward de Rothschild, a member of the French branch of the clan, with:

"I'm honored to meet a Rothschild and trust you're pleased to meet a Fuller."

(Fenner Fuller had some good credentials: One of his ancestors landed on the Mayflower, and his two names derived from forbears who governed Rhode Island.)

He was also the type who could load a garbage-truck driver, disabled by an excess of spirits, back on his truck on Christmas Day and return the cart and cargo to the dumping grounds.

Esther Fuller was and is petite and artistically inclined, and in 1945 selling food would have ranked near the bottom in her listing of occupational preferences.

Fenner and Esther Fuller were looking for a location for an art gallery when they were advised by a prospective landlord that what Oakland needed was a restaurant.

Fenner, who had been the manager of a cafeteria for war workers at Vallejo, decided on the restaurant.

Esther did her best to turn the restaurant into an art gallery. First she painted the walls bright magenta and chartreuse.

"If I was going to have to spend my time in a restaurant," she says, "I decided it should look as little like a restaurant as possible."

The interior was patterned on the old-fashioned dining rooms in inns and the term restaurant was never used in the outside signs designating the business.

Mrs. Fuller thinks the restaurant was the first in Oakland to have music piped into the dining area.

Fenner Fuller's opened with an art exhibit.

"My point," says Mrs. Fuller, "was interesting the public in art without pushing it on them."

Mrs. Fuller, who had been a volunteer worker with the San Francisco Museum of Art, says that at the time culture was on the decline in the Eastbay and artists had very few places to exhibit.

So the walls and shelves and floor of Fenner Fuller's became a showcase for the work of local artists.

The exhibitions changed regularly, but some works were permanent and best remembered by regular patrons. These were the ceramic clowns produced by Fenner Fuller.

He began dabbling with clay one day when he went to visit Esther at the Mills College ceramic shop and the clay turned into a clown.

No matter what he started out to make, he mused one day, it always ended up as a clown.

When he died in April, 1964, he left a collection of more than 150 clowns. He had given a few to select friends but he turned down numerous offers to sell them.

"They're like children," he said, "every one different."

The interest in clowns, Mrs. Fuller explains, dates back to her husband's New England boyhood when one of his brothers ran away with the circus and Fenner worked a while as a tent manager.

The excitement of the circus and his love of show business never left him, she says.

The restaurant business did little to change either Fenner or Esther Fuller. Nor did the restaurant change.

From its opening it was a creation of the personalities of its operators and as much a home as a restaurant.

The cook, Mrs. Arlillie Sudduth, has been there since the first week.

After her husband's death, Mrs. Fuller says, she kept the restaurant open for the dinner meal only, to keep his name before the public and to serve those customers who dropped by periodically, almost ritually.

Tonight an old customer, Frank Anderson, will celebrate his 95th birthday with his annual party at Fenner Fuller's.

About a month ago, Mrs. Fuller lost the lease.

"It was Fenner's love," she says of the restaurant, "and I've tried to keep it as long as I could. I'm glad it was out of my hands."

Ironically, the space will be taken over for selling television, an instrument that was only a dream in February, 1945, and, some might say, the chief cause of the decline of kinship, graciousness and the way of life that Fenner Fuller's stood for.

www.ingramcontent.com/pod-product-compliance
Lightning Source LLC
Chambersburg PA
CBHW040356010526
44108CB00049B/2932